BELL'S BRITISH THEATRE

SELECTED PLAYS
1791-1802; 1797

Forty-nine plays
unrepresented in editions of
1776-1781 and 1784

In Sixteen Volumes
of which this is
Volume Fifteen

With a New Preface
by Byrne R.S. Fone and with
New Author and Play Indexes

AMS PRESS
NEW YORK

Library of Congress Cataloging in Publication Data

Main entry under title:

Selected plays from Bell's British Theatre.

Consists of reprints of plays published separately by J. Bell and G. Cawthorn, London, between 1791 and 1802.

Includes indexes.

CONTENTS: v. 1 Bickerstaff, I. The school for fathers. Bickerstaff, I. The Hypocrite, altered from Colley Cibber. Bickerstaff, I. The plain dealer, altered from William Wyncherley. — v. 2 Cibber, C. Love makes a man. Thomson, J. Edward and Eleonora. Griffiths, E. School for rakes. — v.3. Colman, G. The jealous wife. Colman, G. Bonduca, altered from Beaumont and Fletcher. Kendrick, W. Falstaff's wedding. |etc.|

1. English drama — 18th century. I. Bell, John, 1745-1831. British Theatre.

PR1269.S4   1977   822'.6'08   76-44553
ISBN 0-404-00840-2

Reprinted from the edition of 1792, London
First AMS edition published in 1977
Manufactured in the United States of America

International Standard Book Number:
Complete Set: 0-404-00840-2
Volume Fifteen: 0-404-00855-0

AMS PRESS INC.
NEW YORK, N.Y.

CONTENTS

PREFACE

The plays of Samuel Foote (1720-1777), though in fact closer to farce than comedy, were popular because they were controversial and often libelous. He satirized living people with careless abandon, and so devised his plays that they gave him a chance to use on stage his great gifts of mimicry and impersonation. His career as an actor and as an astonishing mimic was successful enough so that he was able to build the new Haymarket theater. His works include skits like *Taste* (1752) and farcical comedies, among which are *The Minor* (1760) in which he satirizes the Methodist George Whitefield and *The Patron* (1764) in which he attacks the ridiculous "Bubb" Dodington. Thus his plays are vehicles for personal imitation rather than for drama.

Robert Dodsley (1703-1764) rose from a footman to be a bookseller and publisher of most of the major authors of his time. In between he was a poet and playwright, and was a man of some taste and enterprise. The author of *The Muse in Livery*, poems by a footman poet, he produced between the years 1735 and 1758 half a dozen theatrical pieces of which *The Toy-Shop* was the most popular. His tragedy, *Cleone* was, however, an academic effort, and is lost in the welter of other plays like it.

Richard Glover, whose plays are commented on earlier in these volumes, contributed the deservedly forgotten *Medea*, which some apparently considered memorable in its time.

Thornthwaite sculp.

Mrs SIDDONS as MEDEA.

I once had Parents— Ye endearing names!
How my torn heart with recollection bleeds!

London Printed for J. Bell British Library Strand Feb.y 8.1792.

BRITISH

MEDEA.

Thea.   *The injured daughter of Æetes.*
Thou mayst discover thro' those parting boughs.
A.12   Scene I.

Hamilton pinxt.   Grignion sculp.

London. Printed for J. Bell. British Library. Strand. Feby. 18. 1792.

MEDEA.

A

TRAGEDY,

BY MR. GLOVER.

ADAPTED FOR

THEATRICAL REPRESENTATION,

AS PERFORMED AT THE

THEATRE-ROYAL, DRURY-LANE.

REGULATED FROM THE PROMPT-BOOK,

By Permission of the Manager.

"The Lines distinguished by inverted Commas, are omitted in the Representation."

LONDON:

Printed for the Proprietors, under the Direction of
JOHN BELL, British Library, STRAND,
Bookseller to His Royal Highness the Prince of Wales.

MDCCXCII.

MEDEA.

THIS is the last produced of four plays by different authors upon the same subject. For those previous to the present, it is enough to stile them bad translations of a bad original—they are all from SENECA.

Mr. GLOVER however has taken a scope less servile and better suited to his powers; for though he has kept SENECA constantly in his eye, yet his poem bears very frequent marks of originality and skill.

It does not in truth appear designed for the stage under our present modes of thinking, retaining so much of the declamatory sentiment and the unmanagable chorus of SENECA.—We do not recollect its performance more than for the benefits of an ACTRESS of great merit—the late Mrs. YATES.

In the closet it will give pleasure to such as are fond of the ANCIENT DRAMA; a Greek subject in the dress of a Roman poet, modernized a little by an English writer of considerable merit.

A ij

PROLOGUE.

THOUGH *wild our theme, the grave historian's page*
Hath sanctify'd the tale through ev'ry age.
Who hath not heard of Argo sent from Greece,
Of Jason's labours for the golden fleece,
And fond Medea's ill-requited aid
To that false hero, who his vows betray'd?
In ev'ry clime, where learned Muses reign,
The stage hath known Medea's mournful strain;
Hath giv'n the flying car, and magic rod,
To her, th' avowed descendant of a god.

The storms of trouble, which afflict the great,
Teach private life to prize its tranquil state.
That truth the moral of our fable shows
Too well in scenes of unexampled woes,
Which here will ravage an exalted breast,
Of merit conscious, and with shame opprest;
Where love and fury, grief and madness join'd,
O'erturn the structure of a godlike mind.
Pow'r, wisdom, science, and her birth divine,
In vain to shield her from distress combine:
Nor wisdom, pow'r, nor science yield relief;
Her potent wand can vanquish all, but grief:

In vain her winged chariot sweeps the air,
To shun that mightier sorceress, despair.

  The characters and passions hence exprest
Are all submitted to the feeling breast;
Let ancient story justify the rest.

Dramatis Personae.

DRURY - LANE.

Men.

JASON,	- Mr. Smith.
Æson,	- Mr. Palmer.
Creon,	- Mr. Bensley.
LYCANDER,	- Mr. Farren.
First Colchian,	- Mr. Packer.
First Corinthian,	- Mr. Griffiths.

Women.

MEDEA,	- Mrs. Yates.
THEANO,	- Mrs. Hopkins.
HECATE,	- Mr. Bransby.
First Phæacian.	

Colchians, Phæacians, Thessalians, *and* Corinthians.

SCENE *in the citadel of* Corinth, *between a grove sacred to* Juno, *and the royal palace, with a distant prospect of the sea.*

MEDEA.

ACT I. SCENE I.

LYCANDER *seeing* THEANO *advancing from the Temple of* JUNO.

Lycander.

THAT form divine, by all rever'd and lov'd,
Moves from the temple. On her pensive brow
Sits holy care with gentleness and grace,
Whose placid beams humanity reveal.
She stops contemplating the sea. Theano—
Why with that musing aspect tow'rd the main
Stand'st thou regardless of thy brother's voice?

Thea. Imperial Juno in an awful vision,
This morn presented to my wondring sight
The shapes of strangers by distress pursu'd;
Whom to the refuge of this holy place
I must receive obedient to her charge:
And lo! a vessel turns her hast'ning prow
To Corinth's harbour.

Lyc. Ten well measur'd strokes
Of her swift oars will reach the shore below :
But hear my errand.   Creon knows, thy altar
Unclad with garlands still proclaims thy firmness
Against his daughter's marriage; then prepare
Thy hallow'd eye to meet his threat'ning brow;
Fence thy chaste ear against his impious vaunts,
Which urge th' example of Almighty Jove
For his own thirst of empire.

   Thea. Say to Creon,
Kings should aspire to imitate the gods,
Not in their pow'r, but goodness; human virtues
More nigh to Heav'n's perfection may be rais'd,
Than human grandeur : Jove derides the toil
Of mortal pow'r, but smiles on righteous deeds.

   Lyc. Thus would I speak, Theano, could my words
And thoughts be tun'd in harmony like thine;
But danger breaks that union in a palace,
And strains the tongue to discord with the heart :
Then pacify thy goddess, when the king
Exacts my service, if discretion wears
A mask of duty; kindly thou impute
Blame to my station, and absolve Lycander.

   But look; yon vessel hath discharg'd its train,
Who climb the hill with aged steps and slow.

   Nay, turn thy eyes; a second troop of strangers
March through the city.   Sable is their garb,
Their mien dejected.   This demands my care.
Farewell.   [*Exit.*

Enter Colchians.

Thea. What forms are these ? All-potent goddess !
I feel thee now ; my vision is accomplish'd.

    1 *Colc.* O thou, who seem'st the guardian of these
        shades,

Which from the isthmus shew their tow'ring growth,
The sailor's guide through Corinth's double main ;
Permit an humble stranger to enquire,
What pow'r is worshipp'd here.

    Thea. The very garb !
The figures painted in my recent vision !   [*Aside.*

    Thy feet, O stranger, stand on sacred earth.
These shades enclose the venerable fane
Erected there to hymeneal Juno,
Whose presence guards the citadel of Corinth.

    1 *Colc.* Then let us lift our suppliant voice unblam'd,
That in the refuge of this hallow'd grove
Our exil'd feet may rest.

    Thea. Your suit is granted.
So wills the pow'r inhabiting that temple.
And say, ye favour'd of connubial Juno,
What are your names and country ?

    1 *Colc.* From the banks
Of distant Phasis, and the Euxin wave,
Lost to our native mansions, are we come,
Ill-guided Colchians, to the walls of Corinth.
On king Æetes' daughter we attend,
That boast of Asia, to the sun ally'd,

To Hecaté and Circé, more illustrious
In her own virtues, for her wisdom known
Through every clime, the all-endow'd Medea.

 Thea. Where is your princess?

 1 *Colc.* In that anchor'd bark,
Which to your haven from Iolcos sail'd;
Where, on his specious embassy to Creon,
Her husband left her on a lonely pillow.
At length, impatient of his tedious absence,
She and her sons have brav'd th' unsparing deep.

 Thea. Yet more unsparing, than the deep, is man.
So will this daughter of affliction find,
When her sad feet are planted on this shore.

 1 *Colc.* How swift are evil tidings! While our keel
But lightly touch'd that well-frequented strand,
We heard, th' ungrateful Jason would divorce her,
This day, to wed the daughter of your monarch.

 Thea. If Heav'n prevent not. Through the solemn
   shade
Direct thy view. That high rais'd altar note
Close by the fountain. Thither lead your princess.
This is a refuge, which no regal pride
High-swoll'n with pow'r, nor multitude inflam'd
By madding discord, nor invader's rapine
Have e'er profan'd. Return. Yon palace opens.
No friend of yours approaches. It is Creon.
Thou too be present, goddess, and illumine
The earth-born darkness of thy servant's mind.

       [*Exeunt* Colchians.

Enter CREON.

Creon. Why do they paint Medea's woes to me ?
A king should lift his steady front on high,
And, while he gazes on the radiant throne,
Where bright ambition sits amid the stars,
The hopes, the fears, the miseries of others
Pass by unheeded in his contemplation.
    Art thou come forth with those ill-omen'd looks
To blast the public festival ?
    Thea. Howl, howl,
Deluded city ; banish from thy dwellings
The genial banquet ; fill thy streets with mourners
To celebrate in notes of lamentation
A nuptial day offensive to the gods.
    Creon. Think'st thou, thy priestly office can avail
To counteract the high designs of kings ?
Go, and with bridal chaplets deck thy altar,
Lest thou provoke me to confound thy pride
Elate with wreaths of sanctity in vain.
    Thea. Not that the holy fillet binds my temples,
Not, that before the altar I present
The public victim, or a nation's vows
By me are usher'd to th' eternal thrones,
Misjudging monarch, is my heart elate ;
It is, that virtue owns me for her servant.
Benevolence and pity guide my will,
Beneficence and charity my deeds.
Ev'n now, though deem'd importunate and proud,

2

My soul bows down in heaviness for Creon,
And at his danger sighs in mournful warnings.

Creon. Repeat thy warnings to the coward's ear.
My danger ?

Thea. From that goddess, who inspir'd
The Colchian princess to desert her father,
To aid the Grecian heroes, and restore
Our lost possession of the golden fleece.
The voice of loud complaint from yonder beach
Already strikes her ear. Medea——

Creon. Ha !
What of Medea ?

Thea. Is arriv'd in Corinth.

Creon. Arriv'd !

Thea. She and her children, to reclaim
A husband and a father in that prince
Whom thou hast destin'd to Creüsa's bed.

Creon. Thou, who obtain'st infinity of pow'r,
Lord of Olympus, king of gods and men,
Dost thou regard thy sceptred sons below ?
Say, shall a female hand o'erturn the basis,
Which I am founding to enlarge my sway ?
If so, resume the diadem I wear;
Its scanty circle I reject with scorn.

Thea. Ye winds, disperse impieties like these;
Nor let their sound profane the heav'nly threshold.

Creon. Hence to thy temple.

Thea. Thou defy'st not me,
But her, whose awful presence fills that temple.

Imperfect victims, inauspicious off'rings,
And sounds portentous have foboded long
Her high displeasure. Her apparent form
Stood near my pillow at the op'ning dawn,
And strictly charg'd me to receive this stranger.
Think too, what lofty science arms Medea
With more than nature's force.

   Creon. I think it false,
And all the fabled wonders of her charms,
Thy legends too of inauspicious off'rings,
Imperfect victims, and portentous sounds,
What priests may publish, and a king despise.
Hence to the temple.

   Thea. Farewell, rash prince. My duty is discharg'd.

   Creon. Stay. Dost thou mean to give this Colchian
      refuge?

   Thea. Can I dispute a deity's injunction?

   Creon. Go, dream again; procure some wiser vision,
Which may instruct thee to avoid my wrath.

                    [*Exit* Theano.

Enter LYCANDER.

   Creon. Where hast thou loiter'd to conceal th' ar-
      rival
Of this accurst enchantress, and the purpose
Of thy rebellious sister to protect her?

   Lyc. My lord, these tidings are to me unknown;
But further news of high import I bear.
Iolchian Æson, Jason's royal sire,
Advancing now, anticipates this notice.

B

Enter Æson, *with* Thessalians *in mourning.*

Creon. Thrice hail! my double brother. Do I
    owe
Thy timely presence to our ancient friendship,
Or to th' alarm, Medea's flight might raise,
Who scarce precedes thy fortunate appearance?
    My sudden joy o'erlook'd that dusky robe.
    Æs. It suits my fortune. Heavy with affliction,
My weary feet are banish'd from Iolcos.
How my fell brother, Pelias, that usurper
Of my paternal sway, was foil'd and slain,
Thou know'st. His son retreated into Thrace;
Whence he hath pour'd a savage host of ruffians,
With unexpected inroad, and so rapid,
That instant flight alone preserv'd thy friend,
Thy suppliant now for aid.
    Creon. Dismiss thy cares.
Soon shall thy warlike son display his banners,
Extend my frontier, and recover thine.
More of thy fortunes shalt thou tell hereafter;
But give to gladness this selected day
Of Jason's nuptials.
    Æs. Nobly thou reliev'st
A king's distress. Now satisfy the parent.
Lead me to Jason.
    Creon. Follow to my palace.
    Lyc. He is not there.
    Creon. What say'st thou?
    Lyc. On the sands

Alone with melancholy pace he treads,
As I but now descry'd him from this rock.

   Æs. With melancholy pace?

   Creon. His promise binds him
This very morning to espouse Creüsa.

   Æs. Perhaps with fresh calamity o'erworn,
I doubt too much; yet hear me.

   Creon. Thy appearance
Removes all doubts. Lycander, find the prince.
Say, who is come to celebrate his nuptials.

   Æs. [*To* Lycander.] Is he a stranger to Medea's
       landing?

   Lyc. I trust he is.

   Æs. They must not meet.

   Creon. Lycander,
See, thou prevent it. Send Theano to us;
And let her bring obedience: else her fault
Shall on thy head be punish'd.   [*Exit* Lyc.

   Æs. Should my son
Once see Medea!

   Creon. Can her looks annul
A league like ours?

   Æs. Alas! thou little know'st her.
Her eyes surpasses that refulgent star,
Which first adorns the evening; and her talents
Exceed her beauty. " Like the forked thunder
" She wields resistless arguments; her words
" With more than lightning's subtlety are wing'd."

   Creon. Why art thou startled?

   Æs. She is there—ascending;

B ij

My sight, acquainted with her haughty steps,
Shrinks, ere they touch the summit of this hill.

 Creon. Which is the far-fam'd sorceress of Colchis?

 Æs. Too well distinguish'd by her stately port,
And elevation o'er that weeping train,
She tow'rs a genuine offspring of the gods.
Rage on her brow, and anguish in her eye,
Denounce the growing tempest of her mind.

 Creon. Now, god of waters, since thy partial hand
Thrusts this barbarian outcast on my shores,
Back to thy floods the fugitive I spurn.

 Æs. What means my royal friend? Retire. Avoid
This formidable woman, who may wound
Our dignity. I know her soaring mind,
Which, all enlighten'd with sublimest knowledge,
Disdains the state and majesty of kings,
Nor ranks with less than deity itself.

 Creon. Curse on her beauty, and majestic mien!
But let the rumour of her pow'r be true;
The Sun, her boasted ancestor, may arm
Her hand with fire; let Hecaté and Circé,
The goddesses of spells, and black enchantments,
Attend her steps, and clothe her feet in terror:
We have our fiends; the sorceress shall find,
That grief, despair, distraction wait our nod,
To wring her heart through all her magic guards.

[Exeunt.

 Enter MEDEA, *her two Children,* Colchians *and*
Phæacians.

 Med. No more, I charge you. Noble minds, op-
  press'd

By injuries, disdain the sound of comfort.

Ye fiends and furies, wont to leave your flames
At my command, and tremble at my charms,
Now, now ascend, and aid Medea's rage.
Give me the voice of thunder to resound
My indignation o'er the earth and heav'ns;
That I, who draw my lineage from the Sun,
Am fall'n below the basest lot of slaves:
That anguish, want, despair, contempt and shame,
Are heap'd together by the hands of fate,
Whelm'd in one mass of ruin on my head,
And dash my struggling virtue to the ground.

　1 *Colc.* Why to our faithful counsels art thou deaf?

　Med. Canst thou by counsel waft my exil'd feet
To my lost parents, my forsaken friends,
And native palace?—Oh! I gave him all;
To him my virgin bosom I resign'd,
For him the regal mansion of my father,
The lov'd companions of my youth deserted;
From foul defeat, from shame, from death I sav'd
　　　him:
What more could woman?—Yet he weds another.
Me he abandons, and these helpless infants,
Forlorn, unshelter'd in a foreign clime,
To ev'ry outrage, ev'ry want expos'd.

　" Blast his perfidious head, vindictive lightnings!
" Unhappy woman! Canst thou, in the height
" Of thy despair, thy rage and indignation,
" Canst thou pursue him with a heavier curse,
" Than to be plung'd in woes, which equal thine?"

1 *Colc.* Though stung with just resentment, due
     regard
Pay to my age, fidelity and service.
A long and painful traverse from Iolcos
Hast thou endur'd, nor since thy landing here,
The needful succour known of rest, or food.

    Med. Talk not to me of nourishment and rest.
Food to these lips, and slumber to these eyes,
Must ever now be strangers.

     1 *Colc.* By the beams
Of thy forefather, never will I see
Thy wisdom bound in vassalage to passion.
Once more I warn thee, princess, to thy refuge.
This is the consecrated bow'r of Juno.
Thou underneath the hospitable shade
Sit suppliant down.

     Med. Improvident Medea!
To raise another from destruction's depths,
To wealth, to glory raise him, yet thyself
Leave destitute and suppliant! Oh! what art thou,
Whom blinded men unerring wisdom call?
Thou couldst not pierce the thin, the airy veil,
Which from my eyes conceal'd the paths of danger;
Nor canst thou now repel th' increasing storm
Of rapid anguish, which o'erturns my peace:
Down to the endless gloom of dreary night;
Hence, let me drive thee from my inmost soul,
That nothing calm may hover nigh my heart
To cool its pain, and save me from distraction. [*Exit.*

    " *A Colc.* Come on, ye soft companions in affliction,

" Melodious daughters of Phæacia's isle ;

" In strains alternated let us chant our grief :

" Perhaps our mistress we may charm to rest.

" *A Phæa.* O music, sweet artificer of pleasure,

" Why is thy science exercis'd alone

" In festivals, on hymeneal days,

" And in the full assemblies of the happy ?

" Ah ! how much rather should we court thy skill

" In sorrow's gloomy season, to diffuse

" Thy smooth allurements through the languid ear

" Of self-devour'd affliction, and delude

" The wretched from their sadness.

" *A Colc.* Let us melt

" In tuneful accents flowing to our woes ;

" That so Medea may at least reflect,

" She is not singly wretched. Let her hear

" Our elegies, whose measur'd moan records

" Our friends forsaken, and our country lost ;

" That she no longer to her sole distress

" Her deep-revolving spirit may confine,

" But by our sorrows may relieve her own.

" *First part of the music.* [*Iambics.*

" *A Colc.* Ye stately battlements and tow'rs,

" Imperial Corinth's proud defence ;

" Thou citadel, whose dewy top

" The clouds in fleecy mantles fold,

" Projecting o'er the briny foam

" An awful shadow, where the might

" Of Neptune urges either shore,

" And this contracted isthmus forms :

" Ah! why your glories to admire
" Do we repining Colchians stand,
" Ill-fated strangers! on the banks
" Of silver-water'd Phasis born.

" [*Trochaics.*

" *A Phæa.* Pride of art, majestic columns,
" Which beneath the sacred weight
" Of that god's refulgent mansion
" Lift your flow'r-insculptur'd heads;
" Oh! ye marble channell'd fountains,
" Which the swarming city cool,
" And, as art directs your murmurs,
" Warble your obedient rills :
" You our eyes obscur'd by sorrow
" View unconscious of your grace,
" Mourning still our lost Phæacia,
" Long-remember'd native isle.

" [*Iambics.*

" *A Phæa.* O that on fam'd Peneus' banks
" The nymphs of Pelion had bemoan'd
" Their shady haunts to ashes turn'd
" By Heav'n's red anger! hateful pines,
" Which form'd thy well-compacted sides,
" O Argo, fatal to our peace.
" Thou never then through Adria's wave
" Hadst reach'd Phæacia's blissful shore,
" Nor good Alcinöus the hand
" Of Jason with Medea join'd,
" Nor sent us weeping from our homes,
" Her luckless train, to share her grief.

" *Second Part.* [*Trochaics.*

" *A Phæa.* Known recesses, where the echoes
  " Through the hollow-winding vale,
" And the hill's retentive caverns
  " Tun'd their voices from our songs;
" Shade-encircled, verdant levels,
  " Where the downy turf might charm
" Weary feet to joyous dances
  " Mix'd with madrigals and pipes:
" O ye unforgotten pleasures,
  " Pleasures of our tender youth,
" You we never shall revisit,
  Ill-exchang'd for scenes of wo.

  " *A Colc.* From the polish'd realms of Greece,
Where the arts and muses reign,
" Truth and justice are expell'd.
" Here from palaces and tow'rs
" Snowy-vested faith is fled;
" While beneath the shining roofs
" Falsehood stalks in golden robes.
" Dreary Caucasus! again
" Take us to thy frozen breast;
" Let us shiver on thy ridge,
" Ever-during pile of ice
" Gather'd from the birth of time!
  " *A Phæa.* Cheering breeze with sportive pinion
  " Gliding o'er the crisped main,
" With our tresses thou shalt wanton
  " On our native sands no more.
" Fountains, whose melodious waters,

" Cooling our Phæacian grots,
" Oft our eyes to sweetest slumber
   " With their lulling falls beguil'd;
" We have chang'd your soothing warble
   " For the doleful moan of wo,
" And, our peaceful moss deserting,
   " Found a pillow thorn'd with care.   [*Exeunt.*"

ACT II. *SCENE I.*

JASON *advancing from the End of the Stage,* THEANO
on one Side, MEDEA *in the Grove.*

Theano.

THE princely steps of Jason are in sight.
He scarce conjectures, that th' indignant breast
Of her he injures, pours from yonder shades
Its high-ton'd anguish.   Yet, illustrious false one,
What stinging thoughts distort thy manly frame!
How have thy gestures lost their wonted grace
In this keen struggle with upbraiding conscience!
Thou soon, before that inward judge arraign'd,
Shalt hear me plead thy wrong'd Medea's cause.

   " This is the crisis——— Too complacent hero,
" By pride untutor'd, though misled by error,
" Thou wilt be calm and gentle to rebuke."

   Jas. Press'd by a father's absolute decree,
Solicited by Corinth's potent lord,
Aw'd with the specious sound of public good,

I have consented, and the hour is nigh.

Oh ! in some future hour of sad reflection

May not my heart with self-reproach confess,

This plea of public welfare was ambition ;

And filial duty was a feeble tie

To authorise the breach of sacred vows.

    Med. [*In the grove.*] Ungrateful Jason !

    Jas. Whence proceeds this voice ?

    Med. [*In the grove.*] Oh, sire of light, thou seest my
         wrongs.

    Jas. Again !

Imagination, pregnant with remorse,

In sounds unreal yields its birth of terror.

    Med. [*In the grove.*] Ye arbiters of oaths, and plight-
         ed faith,

O Jove and Themis, hear !

    Jas. It is a voice !

Resembling hers, when she, alas ! is far ;

No mockery of fancy.   [*Leans against the scene.*

    Thea. [*Advancing.*] On his cheek

Health seems to wither. O'er his shaded sight

The shiv'ring eye-lids close. A creeping tremor

O'erspreads his fading lips, and dewy limbs.

Bless'd be these signals of returning virtue.

    Hail ! prince. Why stand'st thou list'ning ? What
         alarms thee ?

    Jas. An awful murmur from offended heav'n,

Through yonder branches, issu'd in a voice,

Which chill'd my spirit, and unnerv'd my strength.

    Thea. What didst thou hear ?

Jas. Medea's well-known accents
Thrice did the vocal prodigy repeat,
Though seas divide her from these faithless arms.

    Thea. There is no need of prodigy. Mere nature
In thy own breast will startle, when thou know'st,
It was Medea's self, who call'd on Jason.

    Jas. Herself?

    Thea. The injur'd daughter of Æetes,
But newly-wafted from Thessalia's shore,
Thou may'st discover through those parting boughs;
Where she is seated near the fountain's brink
With her pale cheek reclining on the altar.

    Jas. [*Looking on the grove.*] Stern deities of ven-
         geance, and of justice!
Now pass your sentence, Nemesis and Thamis!
My ill-wrought web of hated life unravel,
Which was not wove for happiness.

    Thea. Be patient.

    Jas. Peculiar woes through ev'ry stage of being
Were Jason's portion. Early I beheld
My father's crown usurp'd. My youth subjected
To an insidious tyrant was devoted
A sacrifice in Colchis—So he hop'd,
And I wish now!—I triumph'd—Glory follow'd,
The source of new calamity to me.
Where is that glory? Serving selfish kings,
Abetting falsehood, perjury and fraud.

    Thea. Turn thy attention from thy own distress,
To feel, what others suffer by thy frailty,
Thy wife and offspring. Listen.

Jas. I obey.

Thea. How couldst thou lead this all-excelling
        princess
From clime to clime, th' associate in thy toils,
To fall the victim in a foreign land
Of those unrighteous statutes, which appoint
Imperious husbands masters of divorce;
How think, th' establish'd practice of the Greeks,
Or all, which varnish'd policy might plead,
Could e'er absolve thee from a solemn tie,
With such uncommon obligations bound,
By those superior, those unwritten laws,
Which honour whispers to the conscious heart?

Jas. O venerable woman, lend thy aid.

Thea. Atone thy fault. Repentance is heroic,
And holds its rank among the manly virtues.

Jas. Yes, I renounce Creüsa, and her kingdom.
Yet see this breast with new-born terror beat.
Not all my trials through unnumber'd dangers,
From monsters, famine, from the raging deep,
And dark-brow'd care, have so confirm'd my courage,
But that I tremble at th' impending conflict.
" I dread that scorn and fury, whose excess
" May kill repentance, and provoke destruction."

Enter LYCANDER.

Lyc. The king, Theano, summons thee before him.

Thea. What time?

Lyc. This instant.

Thea. I obey his pleasure.

Jas. Thou wilt not leave me ?

Thea. Thou hast heard this summons.
Heed my last words.   Maintain thy just resolves.
Lycander, let thy conduct leave no room
For my reproaches, and the wrath of Juno.

Lyc. Fear not ; thy counsels shall be treasur'd here.

                     [*Exit* Theano.

" I see a sudden change.   My single charge
" I will deliver, and forbear enquiry."

Long have I sought thee, prince.   The royal Æson
Is now in Corinth, and will soon accost thee.

Jas. My father here !   Why, multiply distress,
Accumulate perplexity and shame
On my devoted head, ye righteous pow'rs !

Lyc. Prince, he is near ; and I return to Creon.

                         [*Exit.*

Enter ÆSON.

Jas. Amaz'd, distracted, tortur'd, I retain
My veneration here.   O sacred head,
What from thy peaceful habitation calls
Thy silver hairs to these abodes of wo ?
Or com'st thou wrapt in sable to lament
Our mutual errors, and dishonour'd names ?

Æs. Why I am here, why bearing this apparel,
Too soon will Jason know.   But first reply ;
Why on the sea's waste margin was my son
Observ'd to trace his solitary path ;
When Corinth pauses in her gen'ral gladness,
Her choral songs and minstrelsy suspending
For Jason's absence ?

           1

Jas. Better she should wait,
Whole ages wait, than justice be suspended,
And the return of honour be unwelcom'd.

Æs. Can I interpret these mysterious words?

Jas. Hast thou not heard, my father, that Medea
Weeps in that bow'r, invoking Jove and Themis
To witness what returns she meets from Jason?

Æs. What most I dreaded. Then my aged limbs
Must wear these garments still unchang'd, thy country,
Thy friends, thy father's house unceasing mourn.
The woes of exile more severe, than time,
Indent the furrows deeper on these brows.

Jas. The woes of exile?

Æs. Yes, the race of Pelias
Force me to Corinth. Young Acastus reigns.
The gen'rous Creon promises his aid;
That aid will Jason cruelly prohibit.

Jas. Then we begin to reap the bitter harvest
From seeds, which selfish policy had sown.
When I was hurry'd to these fatal walls,
And, gall'd with jealous fear, Medea left thee;
Heav'n, in that period, from the roll of fortune
Eras'd our titles, and the with'ring sceptre
Shrunk from thy grasp.

Æs. Nay, look not thus entranc'd.
What draws thy eye?

Jas. She rises from the grove,
A sun disfigur'd by a mist of sorrow
Rais'd from our crime. Awake thee—What remains,

C ij

But that we fall before our known protectress,
Confessing both in Jove's offended sight,
How much of weak inconstancy hath stain'd
My name of hero, what ignoble guile
Disgrac'd thy regal head?

   Æs. And who must save Iolcos?

   Jas. She. Medea's gen'rous wisdom,
Which in itself contains the strength of armies,
And quell'd old Pelias, can dethrone the son.

   Æs. What frenzy guides thee? Follow me to Creon.

   Jas. Rest thou with me.

   Æs. Inhuman! dost thou covet
To see my age and dignity revil'd?
I charge thee, follow.

   Jas. Riveted, I wait,
As if congenial with this rock I grew
From its foundations, till Medea come.

   Æs. Revolter! she is coming—But my eye
Shall not be far. Remember, thou dost hazard
Thy country's love, perhaps thy father's too. [*Exit.*

    Enter MEDEA, Colchians *and* Phæacians.

   Jas. How shall I face her injur'd worth, how choose
The most auspicious moment to accost her?

   Med. Why have I science to command the moon,
To draw the spirits from the realms of night,
And trace the hidden pow'rs of baneful nature?
Why am I wise, unless to feel my sorrows
With sharper sensibility, and prove,
How weak is wisdom struggling with despair?

1 *Colc.* Its succour yet solicit. Wisdom smooths
Each thorny path, and Virtue is her sister.

Med. Old man, be silent. Hath Medea's grief
The leisure now to hear thy moral tale?
No, let me loath my being, " curse the sun,
" My bright forefather," and upbraid the heav'ns,
That I was ever born. I will exclaim;
I will demand, ye unrelenting pow'rs,
Why your injustice terrifies the earth
With such an image of distress as mine.

Jas. This interview I see in all its terrors;
But further pause will turn suspense to madness.
Medea—I am come————

Med. And dar'st thou come,
With that unmatch'd ingratitude and falsehood,
To face the constant worth, thou now betray'st?

Jas. I come to lay my errors in thy view.

Med. No, to my view display Creüsa's beauty;
Dwell on her merit, who excels Medea.

Jas. The deity, presiding o'er that temple,
I call to witness, that my father's pleasure————

Med. And dost thou urge thy father, thou perfidious?
Thy father! oh! that I had been thus wise,
And ne'er forgot the duty of a child.

Thy father gave thee a precarious being,
In its first flight of glory doom'd to fall,
Fresh in its prime, a victim to oblivion,
Had not I sav'd and borne thee to renown.

Jas. Jason's life and glory are thy gifts.

Med. I gave thee too my love, my virgin love,

My friends, my country, my unspotted fame,
My joy, my peace, all, all on thee bestow'd;
What could a father more? Him too my pow'r
Snatch'd from oppression, and his treach'rous brother,
Usurping Pelias slew, that cruel Pelias,
Who on thy youth impos'd the dang'rous toil,
Whence I preserv'd thee—But, my wrath, be still.
Inconstant, base alike, both son and sire
Deserve my scorn.

    Jas. Shall contumelious harshness
Blot those perfections from the son deriv'd,
And not one moment to thy wisdom yield,
That thou may'st hear me?

    Med. No, thou most ingrate
Of all, who e'er forgot their benefactors.
When the fam'd Argo, fraught with Grecian princes,
Pierc'd with its beak the sandy verge of Phasis,
What daring hand but mine their trophies rais'd?
The golden fleece amid th' enchanted grove
Had hung untouch'd beside its scaly guardian;
Wild dogs and vultures had devour'd your lambs;
Your bones had whiten'd on the Colchian strand.
I fearless stept between the narrow bounds,
Which parted your devoted lives from fate,
With mystic spells entranc'd the sleepless dragon,
Bent to the yoke the brazen-footed bulls,
And gave you safety, victory, and fame.

    Jas. I own thy merits; and the deep remem-
        brance—

    Med. For ever be detested that remembrance.

Curs'd be the skill, which fram'd your fatal bark,
Accurs'd the gale, which fill'd her spreading canvas ;
But doubly curs'd the hour, the hour of ruin,
When first I viewed that smiling treach'rous form,
And fondly trusted to the fair delusion.
" O that amid the terrors of enchantment,
" When, for thy sake, profoundest hell was open'd,
" Some fiend had whirl'd me to the desert pole ;
" Or that the earth, dividing with my charms,
" Low, as her central cavern, had entomb'd me !"

    Jas. I feel thy anguish, daughter of Æetes,
Which would o'erwhelm me, had I less to offer,
Than my repentant heart.

    Med. Thy perjur'd heart,
Foul with ingratitude and guilt. Avaunt,
And give it thy Creüsa; I despise thee.

    Jas. Think, who I am. Though criminal I stand
And mourn my fault, forget not, I am Jason,
By fame in brightest characters recorded.
Deserving thy reproaches, I endur'd them ;
But sure the lustre of my name is proof
Against contempt.

    Med. The recompence of falsehood.

    Jas. Hold, I conjure thee ?—Nay, I will be heard.
When first I sail'd for Corinth, all my purpose
Was to establish, by a league with Creon,
Th' unstable throne of Thessaly, since crush'd
By fierce Acastus. Æson's strict injunction
To wed Creüsa follow'd my arrival ;

When thou wert distant from my sight, and Creon
Would grant his friendship———

   Med. But by thy disgrace.

   Jas. Impatient woman!

   Med. Could a king's protection
Be rank'd with mine, thou weakly-perjur'd man?

   Jas. Thou shalt not stop me, by th' immortal
       gods!
I will proceed—" Intemp'rate passion stifles
" Her breathless voice—Oh, majesty! Oh, wisdom!
" Oh, features once divine! how long shall rage
" Depoil your grace?" No other form of beauty,
No qualities or talents to thy own
Have I preferr'd. By empire's glaring bubble,
By policy's ensnaring voice misled,
Or by mistaken duty to a parent,
I swerv'd from sacred faith. At thy approach
Light flashes through my error; to thy feet
Contrition brings me, no ignoble suppliant:
The scourge of tyrants, vanquisher of monsters,
Thy instrument of glory, now most glorious,
That he subdues himself, implores thy pardon.

   Oh, unadvis'd!—Obdurate!—While I sue,
Thy unforgiving brow returns disdain.
Think of thy children!

   Med. Traitor, dar'st thou name them?

   Jas. Beware; destruction, with a hunter's speed,
Pursues us both. Inextricable snares
Are spreading round us—Ha! be calm—Provoke

Ill fate no further—Weigh in wisdom's balance
The pow'rful obligations, which assail'd me.

 Med. Can they be weigh'd with conquest, life, and
   fame,
The vast profusion of my bounty on thee,
Thou weak, thou blind, insensible, and base?
No, my superior soul shall stoop no more.
Though once from foul defeat and death I sav'd thee,
I will not raise thee from thy grov'ling falsehood.
Let fortune's whole malignity pursue me,
I and my children wretched, as we may be,
Outcast, derided by the barb'rous herd,
Spurn'd by th' unpitying proud, with grim despair,
With beggary and famine, our companions,
Will wander through th' inhospitable world,
Nor ev'n amidst our complicated woes
E'er think of thee, perfidious, but with scorn.
    [*Exeunt* Medea, Colchians *and* Phæacians.

Enter ÆSON.

 Jas. Then let the tempest roar, tyrannic woman,
The billows rise in mountains o'er thy head.

 Æs. Well, thou hast seen her; while thy father's
   eye
Ach'd at the low submission of a hero,
Who with unmollify'd disdain was spurn'd.
Say, will my gentle son persist to court
The fellowship of fury, and abide
The acrimonious taunt, the settled frown,
The still-renew'd upbraiding? Will my Jason

For this to deathless obloquy abandon
His name of hero, while his arm rejects
A proffer'd aid to reinstate his father,
Redeem his country, and refresh his laurels,
With want of action fading?

    Jas. There, O Mars,
Thou dost provide a banquet for despair.

    Æs. No, for thy valour, son, a feast of glory.
Come, leave this melancholy spot.   Return
With me to joy.

    Jas. I go—but never more
Speak to thy son of joy.   My soul forgoes
All gentle thoughts.   Its sad relief is horror
From the grim pow'r of homicide and ravage.

    O that this ev'ning, lighted by the stars,
And glimpse of armour, I might turn my back
On Corinth's bulwarks; that the trumpet's clangor,
The shrill-mouth'd clarion, and the deep-ton'd horn,
The groans of slaughter, and the crash of spears,
Might blend their discord for my nuptial song.
                         [Exeunt.

    " *Enter* Colchians *and* Phæacians *from the Grove, look-*
        " *ing on* Jason, *as he quits the Stage.*

                    " *[Solemn Recitative.*

    " *A Colc.* Thou who didst yoke the brazen-footed
          bulls,

    " And fearless guide the adamantine plough,

    " Which Vulcan labour'd, o'er the direful soil

    " Sown with the serpent's teeth, whence crested helms

" And spears high-brandish'd by the earth-born race

" For thy encounter pierc'd the crumbling mould ;

" Thou conqueror, beware : more dang'rous foes

" Doom'd to subdue thee in that palace wait.

　　　　　　　" [*Trochaics.*

　" *A Phæa.* Soft, alluring wiles are there

" To seduce thee from the paths

" Trod by godlike steps alone,

" Paths of virtue, paths of praise.

" Colchian monsters, syren's songs,

" Might thy mortal frame destroy :

" These will kill thy glorious name ;

" Matchless Jason, then beware.

　　　　　　" [*Solemn Recitative.*

　" *A Colc.* Thou yet untainted hero, Ah! reflect,

" That keenest sorrow, poverty, or pain,

" Are light and gentle to the bitter darts,

" Thrice steep'd in gall, which Nemesis directs

" Against his bosom, who, by merit pass'd,

" Once drew th' enchanting melody of praise,

" Then, forfeiting the sweet report of fame,

" O'er his irrevocable loss repines.

　　　　　　　" [*Trochaics.*

　" *A Phæa.* Shall the nymphs of Tempé's vale,

" Who in rural lays record

" Thy persuasive love, that won

" Kind Medea to thy aid,

" Shall they change th' applauding strain ?

" Shall the discord of reproach

" Wound thy ear, accustom'd long
" To the music of renown ?   [*Exeunt.*"

ACT III. SCENE I.

Enter THEANO *and the* 1 Colchian.

1 *Colchian.*

HOPE in its bud was blasted by her anger.

Thea. Unhappy anger! but her wrongs are great ;
Nor is my pity less. Instruct me, Colchian,
Was she not fam'd for hospitable deeds ?

1 *Colc.* Oft hath her known benignity preserv'd
The Grecian strangers on our barb'rous coast.

Thea. Yet now a Grecian prince denies her shel-
    ter.
Well, introduce me to her.

1 *Colc.* Restless anguish
Will soon transport her hither. Look, she comes.
Here let us watch some interval of calmness.

Thea. Are those her children ?

1 *Colc.* Yes, from Jason sprung.

Thea. They too with intermingling tears enhance
The piteous scene. Thou fair and stately tree,
Who once so proudly didst o'ertop the forest,
What cruel hand despoils thee of thy honours ?
Now dost thou show, as blasted by the lightning,
With all thy tender branches with'ring round.

Enter MEDEA, *her two* Children, Colchians *and*
Phæacians.

Eldest Child. Why fly'st thou from us ? Wherefore
     dost thou frown
Whene'er we name, or ask to see our father?
     Med. You have no father !
     Eldest Child. When we left Iolcos,
Didst thou not tell us, he was here in Corinth ?
Now we have pass'd the frightful sea, what hinders
But we may find him ?
     Med. Never find him more
To you a parent, or to me a husband.
     Eldest Child. Alas ! thou weep'st.
     Med. You too must learn to weep,
Ye destin'd wand'rers in the vale of mourning.
Why do you lift your infant eyes to me ?
Your helpless mother cannot guard your childhood,
Nor bid neglect and sorrow stand aloof.

I once had parents—Ye endearing names !
How my torn heart with recollection bleeds !
You too perhaps o'erflow your aged cheeks,
Rend from your heads the venerable snow
Oft, as your lost Medea is recall'd,
And for a hapless offspring mourn like me.
     1 *Colc.* Heart-breaking sorrow now succeeds to
     rage.
Turn, royal mistress ; see the holy priestess.
     Med. Hail ! most humane.
     Thea. To Juno render praise.

Med. She owes me refuge. Prompted first by Juno,
I left my native Phasis, and convey'd
Back to her favour'd clime the golden fleece.
Thy part was all humanity.

 Thea. Sage princess,
Hear me divulge the menaces of Creon
To drive thee hence. Expect his presence soon.
Fear not his anger. Warranted by Juno,
By my high function, by my nature more,
I gave thee, I continue my protection.

 Med. Turn to these infants thy benignant looks.
Them to secure from trouble, and the terrors
Which gather closely on the steps of time,
Is all their mother's care; at whose entreaty
Do thou receive their innocence in charge:
But leave Medea to her own protection.

 Eldest Child. Our father long hath left us. By thy
   side,
And in thy bosom, we had comfort still.
Wilt thou forsake us?

 Med. We will meet again.
Remove them from me. I can bear no longer
To view those mirrors, which reflect the image
Of my distress, and multiply my pains.

 Thea. Weep not, my children.

 Med. Hide their melting softness;
Lest they dissolve the vigour which must save them.
       [Medea *continues weeping.*

 Thea. Come, lovely mourners, rest a while with me.
Come, and be practis'd to repeat your vows

For this most wrong'd of mothers.   You shall lift
Your blameless hands, sweet supplicants, shall kneel
To nuptial Juno, and to rev'rend Themis,
The arbitress of oaths, and plighted faith.
The dove-like voice of your untainted age,
Thus visited by undeserv'd affliction,
May win their guardian mercy; " when the pray'rs
" Of man, false man, grown reprobate by time,
" With all the pomp of hecatombs, would fail."

        [*Exit to the Temple with the Children.*

  Med. Are they withdrawn?

  1 *Colc.* They are.

  Med. Then, mighty spirit,
Once more at least thy majesty shall blaze
Such as thou wert amid th' enchanted wood ;
When thou didst summon hell's reluctant pow'rs,
And hell obey'd: when dark'ning from her car
The moon descended, and the knotted oak
Bent with thy charms, which tam'd the wakeful dra-
      gon,
And safety gave to demi-gods and heroes.

  1 *Colc.* Behold the King.

    Enter CREON, LYCANDER, *and Attendants.*

  Med. Why comes the king of Corinth
To break upon my sorrows, " and to vaunt,
" That his injustice is endu'd with pow'r
" To grieve Medea ?"

  Creon. To debate, weak woman,

Is thy known province ; to command is mine.
Be seen no longer in the bounds of Corinth.

   Med. And who art thou dost give Medea law,
And circumscribe the slend'rest spot on earth
Against her passage ? Unconfin'd as winds
I range with nature to her utmost bounds;
While, as I tread, mankind reveres my steps,
Its hidden pow'rs each element unfolds,
And mightiest heroes, anxious for renown,
Implore Medea's favour. What is Creon,
Who from the sun's descendant dares withhold
The right to hospitality and justice ?

   Creon. Not of the number who revere thy steps,
Or supplicate thy favour ; one, whose sceptre
Forbids thy residence in Greece. Away ;
Range through the snows of Caucasus ; return
To Pontic deserts, to thy native wilds :
Among barbarians magnify thy deeds.
This land admits no wand'rer like Medea,
Who with a stranger from her father fled,
Fled from her country, and betray'd them both.

   Med. With him I fled, whom thou wouldst foully
        draw
Through blackest treason to thy daughter's bed;
And for the rest, if equity or wisdom
Were Creon's portion, I would plead before him :
But vindicate my actions to a robber,
Who basely watch'd my absence to purloin
My only wealth ! My lofty soul disdains it.

Creon. Hence, while thou may'st, rash woman, ere
　　　thou prove
How strong the awful image of the gods
Is stampt on monarchs, and thou feel my wrath
Swift in destruction like the bolt of Jove.

Med. Dost thou recount thy fables to Medea,
The idiot tale, which cheats the gaping vulgar,
To her who knows the secret source of things?
Behold this comely image of the gods!
This violater of the holiest ties,
Whom the dull hand of undiscerning chance
Hath deck'd in purple robes, and pageant gold,
Resembles much the majesty of heav'n!

Creon. Thy bare expulsion shall not now atone.
I will stand forth th' avenger of Æetes
On his false daughter; for thy crimes in Colchis
Vindictive furies in this distant region,
Shame, chastisement, and insult, shall o'ertake thee,
Spoil that fair body, humble that fell heart;
Till, as with bitt'rest agony it breaks,
Thou curse its wild temerity, which brav'd
The pond'rous hand of majesty incens'd.

Med. Ha! thou vain boaster, hast thou yet to learn
That I can rock the iron throne of Pluto;
Can waft thee struggling to Rhiphæan crags,
Where thou shalt rave, and foam, and gnash thy teeth,
Where frost shall parch thee, where the clouds shall
　　　scatter
Their storms around thee, whirl in sportive air

Thy gorgeous robe, thy diadem and sceptre?
While I—Oh! fruitless, unsubstantial pow'r!
Must still continue wretched—Oh! vain threat!
Hath he not torn my Jason from these arms?
What then avails the knowledge of my mind?
Stretch'd on the rack of anguish is my heart.
What spark of wisdom in my breast remains?
All is extinguish'd there—Oh, Jason! Jason!
                    [*Is supported by her Women.*

 Creon. [*To* Lycander.] Thou seest the haughty sorceress abash'd
Before a monarch's persevering frown.

 Lyc. [*Aside.*] Most injur'd woman!

 Creon. Go, transport her hence,
Ere she revive.

 Lyc. The multitude already
Begin to murmur; were this holy place
Defil'd by force, their zeal would swell to madness.
Perhaps this princess, for her wisdom fam'd,
May be persuaded to abandon Corinth.
And she revives with milder looks.

 Med. [*Aside.*] Pride, pride,
For once be wise; in lowliness disguise thee,
That thou may'st rise to vengeance. King of Corinth,
I only crave three hours to quit thy borders.

 Creon. [*To* Lycander.] If she exceed that slender
  space of time,
Force shall remove her from my loathing sight.
                    [*Exit.*

 Lyc. This contest, princess, thou hast wisely clos'd.

Three hours elaps'd, expect me to return
Thy safe conductor to the kingdom's frontier. [*Exit.*
  1 *Colc.* Thou dost not droop. This tyrant's empty
       threats
Thy very breath could dissipate like clouds,
Which for a while some hideous form assume,
Then pass away dissolv'd to fleeting vapour.
I too will aid thee. By thy father's sister
I was held dear, by Circé, pow'rful queen,
Who taught me various spells and incantations.
  Med. Go then, and bring my wand, that potent rod,
Which grew a branch of ebony, o'ershading
The throne of Pluto ; sever'd thence, and dipt
Thrice in the cold of Lethe's sleepy waters,
By Hecaté on Circé was bestow'd,
By her on me, to still the winds and floods,
Night's drowsy curtains o'er the sky to draw,
And all its active fires entrance to rest.
Leave us apart. Retire, my faithful virgins,
Who share so kindly in Medea's woes.
I would not pierce your gentle hearts with terror.
        [*Exeunt omnes, præter* Med. *and* 1 Colc.
  Med. [*Waving her wand.*] First, rise ye shades im-
       pervious to the sight ;
And you, ye sable-skirted clouds, descend :
Us and our mystic deeds with night surround.
          [*The Stage is darkened.*
Thou, by whose pow'r the magic song   [*Iambics.*
Charms from its orb th' unwilling moon,
Controls the rapid planet's speed,

And dims the constellation's fires;
   " While sounding torrents stop and sleep,
" While fountain-nymphs in dread withhold
" Their mazy tribute from the meads,
" And stiff'ning serpents hear and die :"
   Terrific deity, whose name,
And altar stain'd with human blood
On Tauric cliffs the Scythian wild,
And fell Sarmatian tribes adore;
" Wreath'd in snakes, and twining boughs [*Trochaics.*
" Gather'd from infernal oaks,
" Which o'er Pluto's portal hung
" Shed a second night on hell ;"
   In thy raven-tinɛ̃tur'd stole,
Grasping thy tremendous brand,
With thy howling train around,
Awful Hecaté, ascend.

   1 *Colc.* By the pitchy streams of Styx,
Lethe's mute and lazy flood,
By the dreadful vapour sent
From Avernus' steaming pool ;
   By th' eternal sigh, which heaves
With Cocytus' mournful wave,
By the Phlegethontic blaze,
Direful goddess, hear and rise.
" Or if, where discord late hath heap'd   [*Iambics.*
" Her bloody hecatombs to Mars,
" Thou sweeping o'er the mangled slain
" Dost tinge thy feet in sanguine dew ;
   " Ah! leave awhile the vulture's shriek,

" The raven croaking o'er the dead,
" The midnight wolf's insatiate howl,
" And hither turn thy solemn pace.
   " The winds in magic horror bonnd
" Shall at thy presence cease to breathe,
" No thunder-teeming cloud approach,
" The hoarse and restless surge be dumb."
   Med.   No more.   The strong-constraining spell
      hath tam'd
The restive blast; the pliant leaves are fix'd;
The fountains rest; th' oblivious birds are hush'd;
And dead the billows on the silent beach.
Begone—She comes—I feel the rocking ground,
Its entrails groan—Its shiv'ring surface parts.
Scarce can Ætes' child the sight endure.

[*Ex.* 1 *Colc.*

[Hecaté *rises in long black garments, with a wreath of
   snakes, and oaken boughs on her head, and a torch in
   her hand.*]

   Med.   O my propitious and congenial goddess,
Who thy mysterious science hast diffus'd
Of potent herbs, and necromantic songs
Through my capacious bosom; who so long
Hast been assistant to Medea's triumphs,
Now thou behold'st me vanquish'd by despair.

   Hec.   I know thy suff'rings, daughter; but to close
The wounds of anguish, and assuage despair,
Is not the task of hell.

   Med.   Then give me vengeance.
   Hec.   On whom?

Med. Creüsa ?—No—my high revenge
O'erleaps a trifling maid.   Old Æson ?—No.
He is my hero's father.   But for Creon——

Hec. The hour is nigh, when yonder flood will rage,
This rock be loosen'd, and its structures nod ;
Then shall the fury, discord, and red zeal,
Thrice steep'd in Stygian fires, avenge thy wrongs.
Farewell.

Med. A moment stay—My yielding heart
Must ask—Will Jason ever more be kind ?

Hec. Search not thy fate.

Med. Unfold it, I enjoin thee,
By him, thou dread'st, by Demogorgon's name.

Hec. Against thyself, unhappy, thou prevail'st.
Ere night's black wheels begin their gloomy course,
What thou dost love shall perish by thy rage ;
Nor thou be conscious when the stroke is given :
Then, a despairing wand'rer, must thou trace
The paths of sorrow in remotest climes.

[*She descends.*

Med. Destroy my love ! By me shall Jason die ?
Oh ! insupportable ! O pitying Juno !
Assist me sinking to the ground with anguish.

[*Falls to the ground.*

Enter Colchians *and* Phæacians.

1 *Colc.* The streaming purple of the western sun
Glows on these tow'rs and pinnacles again,
Prevailing o'er the darkness, which the wand
Of our sage mistress rais'd—Dejecting sight !

Thy faithful servant can refrain no longer,
But tears must wash the furrows of his cheeks.

 Med. Ah! how much more my eyes should stream
   in torrents!
Ah! how much stronger should my bosom heave,
And sound its agonies in bitter groans
To the remorseless gods! Destroy my Jason!

          [*Starting up.*
The dear, false hero! Perish first my art.

 1 *Phæa.* " How oft have perjur'd lovers been re-
  recall'd
" By strong enchantment? Check these vain com-
   plaints."
Hast thou not magic to constrain this wand'rer
Back to thy arms?

 Med. I have, but scorn the arts
Which may command his person, not his love.
No, fly to Jason. Let the only charm
Be soft persuasion to attract him hither.

 O he is gentle as the summer's breeze,
With looks and gestures fashion'd by the graces.
The messenger be thou, discreet and good.
Medea's pride shall stoop.

 1 *Colc.* [*Aside.*] I go—though hopeless.

 Med. Mean time will I to yonder wood return,
And some deep-shaded receptacle choose.
There, wrapt in darkness, shall my suff'ring soul
The sense of all its injuries disburthen
In secret murmurs, till its rage be spent. [*Exit.*

 " *A Colc.* Native floods rough with ice [*Cretics.*

" Rushing down mountain-sides,

" Whirling thence broken rocks ;

" Your discordant waves that sweep   [*Trochaics.*

" Harshly o'er their flinty beds,

" Yield a more alluring sound

" Than the gently-trilling notes

" Of the tender Grecian lyre,

" Or the swelling strain diffus'd

" From the music-breathing flute.

    " Native groves hoar with frost,   [*Cretics.*

    " Caverns deep, fill'd with night,

    " Shagged clifts, horror's seat ;

" Oh! to these desiring eyes   [*Trochaics.*

" Lovely is your gloom which lives

" In remembrance ever dear.

" You are brighter than my thoughts,

" Which despondency o'erclouds,

" And in these perfidious climes

" Expectation cheats no more.

    " *A Phœa.* Torrents swell, tempests rage,   [*Cretics.*

    " Danger frowns, pain devours,

    " Grief consumes, man betrays ;

" Such our doom in every clime :   [*Trochaics.*

" Yet among the thorns of life

" Hope attends to scatter flow'rs ;

" And Credulity, her child,

" Still with kind imposture smooths

" Heaving trouble, and imparts

" Moments which suspend despair.

    " Goddess bland, soothing hope,   [*Cretics.*

        " In thy smile I confide,
        " And believe Jason comes.
      " All I see delights my eye ;   [*Trochaics.*
      " Ev'ry sound enchants my ear ;
      " Those rude-featur'd crags are gay ;
      " Winds in notes harmonious blow ;

                              [*Turning to the sea.*

      " Hoarsest billows murmur joy ;
      " And my long-forsaken home
      " Wakes the plaintive muse no more.   [*Exeunt.*"

ACT IV.   SCENE I.

Enter JASON, *and the* 1 Colchian.

Jason.

WHY am I summoned ?
    1 *Colc.* But once more to greet her.
    Jas. And be the mark of scorn.
    1 *Colc.* Remind thee, hero,
Of all thy gen'rous labours ne'er deny'd,
But oft repeated to restore the wretched.
Shall thy distress'd Medea be the first
Thou dost refuse to aid ?
    Jas. It is too late.
She cast me from her, and we now are strangers.
    1 *Colc.* I have been long a traveller with time,
And through unnumber'd evils have I noted
Those born of anger to be most deplor'd.
Thou look'st no longer on that mutual care—

                        E

Your children's welfare.   In the wrathful Jason
Benignity is lost, ev'n nature dead
In the fond father.

   Jas. When I nam'd our children,
Her ear was deafen'd, and her scornful tongue
Was sharpen'd into outrage.

   1 *Colc.* See them here,
The lively patterns of their mother's graces,
And sharers in misfortune.

Enter the Children.

  Eldest Child. Art thou found
At last, my father? In thy search we pass'd
Through frightful waters, and in roaring winds.
Come to our mother, who of thee complains;
And, with a promise never more to leave us,
Speak comfort to her.

   Jas. Comfort!

   1 *Colc.* Dost thou shrink
To see these pledges of a love like hers ?
Oh! thou obdurate, who hast thrown the beauties
Of virtue from thee in thy youthful season,
When ev'ry soft sensation is most warm,
To clasp the cold deformity of guilt !
I have no offspring—Must an old man's eyes
Teach thine their tender lesson? Must a heart,
Which time, and ills, and care might well have sear'd,
Teach thee affection, and a parent's feeling ?

   Jas. Support me rather, than depress me, Colchian.

I sink—My soul, dissolving in affection,
Hath quite unmann'd me.

 Eldest Child. Dost thou grieve to see us?

 Jas. No, my poor boys. My spirit bows before you
In love and rev'rence. These indeed subsist
A common care, exacting all regard.
What shall I say?—Not cruel would I seem,
Not ev'n severe—Yet Colchian, let me ask;
Will she——

 1 *Colc.* Command her, she is all submission.

 Jas. " Amid the woes of separating parents,
" Who like the father can protect the offspring?"
Will she commit them to my charge, that comfort,
Prosperity, and honour, be their portion?

 Eldest Child. Ah! do not take us from our mother's
  arms.

 Youngest Child. From our kind mother. Leave us.

 Eldest Child. Leave us here to weep with her.

 Jas. How constant are these children!
But they were never harass'd by her scorn.

  Enter MEDEA, Colchians, *and* Phæacians.

 Med. [*stopping short.*] The man who knew, and yet
  despis'd my worth,
I see before me— Still, thou restiff heart,
Still dost thou rise tumultuous in my bosom;
Oh! thou must bend.

 Jas. Well, daughter of Æetes;
Lo! I am here obedient to thy call.

 Med. Once was the time, when Jason would have come

   E ij

Uncall'd, unprompted, but by love alone.
Why do I bring the wasted glass of joy
Back to my view! Oh! torture of remembrance!
Oh, Jason! Jason!

  Jas. Speak.

  Med. I cannot speak.

  Jas. [*Aside.*] My spirit yields—this mute distress
        o'erwhelms me.

  Med. It is decreed to separate thy name
From mine for ever—First to all restore me ?
Which I relinquish'd for thee to my country,
The veneration which that country paid me,
My injur'd parents, and their lost affection.
To my untainted virgin fame restore me,
My once-untroubled, unreproaching thoughts.
Impossible—Then hear, and yet be just.

  Jas. [*Aside.*] Oh! that this morning she had thus
        address'd me !

  Med. Not love alone, not Hymen's common ties,
But fame and conquest, mutual toils and hardships,
All, which is marvellous and great, conspir'd
To make us one. What stars in distant skies,
What seas, what shores, unvisited before,
Have we not seen together ? And what perils
Could each inhospitable clime present,
From which Medea hath not sav'd her Jason ?
Our toils at length surmounted, must we part ?
My lord—my husband—father of these boys !
Shame, anguish, desperation, rush upon me !
They bind my heart in adamantine woes!

They weigh me down—They bear me to the earth.

                 [*Kneeling with the Children.*

Thus low behold the issue of the Sun
Imploring pity of the man who scorn'd her.

    Jas. Canst thou, O Juno, from thy neighb'ring
        temple

View this illustrious suff'rer at my feet,
Nor swift destruction from thy altar show'r
On my perfidious head? Why rather, goddess,
" Who hast thy thunder, like thy husband, Jove,"
Didst thou not blast me, when, by furies guided,
I ratify'd but now th' unhallow'd contract?

    Med. [*rising.*] What hast thou said?

    Jas. Creüsa—is my wife.   [*He starts at Medea's*
     looks, then fixes his eyes stedfastly upon her, and, after
     some time, proceeds.]

Medea—Ha! Have sense and motion left her!
Her colour dies, which once outshone the morn!
Those radiant eyes, whose majesty proclaim'd
The Sun's own progeny, withdraw their lustre!
Oh! thou most injur'd, utter thy complaints!
Give words to anger, and to sorrow tears!

    Med. Astonishment! What prodigy is there?
Look yonder!

    1 *Colc.* Go—go, children, to the temple;
Avoid this sight.

       [*The Children are led off by a* Phæacian *to the*
       temple.]

    Med. What wonderful appearance
Floats on the main, and stems the lofty surge?

Jas. O execrable perfidy! which fills " the loveliest
     eyes with tears,"
The noblest heart with pangs, the most enlighten'd
     mind with madness!

Med. See, where yon snowy concave in its bosom,
Collecting all the motion of the winds,
Drives the huge burthen to th' affrighted shore!

Jas. O had the flood, she sees in frantic thought,
Ingulph'd that bark!

Med. [*advancing towards him.*] What art thou, most
     presumptuous,
Who dar'st approach the limits of this region?
Hast thou not heard, that bulls with brazen feet,
And sleepless dragons, guard the fatal soil?
He hears unterrify'd—I ne'er beheld
Such majesty and grace.

Jas. Debas'd, deform'd
By guilt's polluting hand!

Med. He speaks—What music!
He claims the golden fleece—What means this warmth,
Which prompts my hand to give the radiant prize?
But wilt thou prove then constant—ever kind?
I must, I will believe thee.

1 *Colc.* What remorse,
What consternation petrify his frame!
And she grows wilder.

Med. Hark! With flaming throats
The bulls begin to roar! The forest trembles!
And see, the dragon hither points his course!
See, his huge pinions beat the tortur'd air!

His monstrous body rolls the blast before him,
And sails amidst a whirlwind! Dost thou droop?
Be not dismay'd, my hero! Stand behind.
Attend, ye demons, whose contagious breath
Defiles the sun, who chill the fiercest heart,
And lock in drowsy sloth the nerves of strength!

Jas. Assume thy terrors—Moulder me to dust.
Now call thy demons, whose infernal grasp
May snatch and hurl me to my destin'd pains.
Let me be stretch'd on torn Ixion's wheel,
Or chain'd in burning adamant endure
The tooth of vipers, and the scorpion's sting;
Oh! rather, rather, than behold thy suff'rings!

Med. Why art thou pale and languid? Thou art
safe!
The slumb'ring monster drops his scaly wings!
Thine is the fleece—Medea too is thine!

[Jason *throws himself back, and is received by the*
Colchians.]

Confusion and amazement!—Is he vanish'd?
Where am I?—On a rock, a desert cliff,
Which overhangs the unfrequented waves;
No plant, but moss, to hide its craggy sides;
No shelter nigh my tempest-beaten head:
And lo! two infants clinging to my knees,
Who join my grief, and call Medea mother!
O thou false hero, whither art thou fled?
Hark—The wind only answers my complaint,
It is the sea, which murmurs to my groans!
Ha! what art thou, grim shape embru'd with gore?

Why dost thou wave that Stygian torch around?
Art thou Revenge from Tartarus enlarg'd
To aid Medea? Come then, shake thy brand
Before my steps! To perpetrate thy mischief,
The winds shall lend their swiftness, hell its fiends,
The sea its fury, and the Sun his flames!   [*Exit.*

    1 *Colc.* Resume thy courage.
    Jas. Yes, my soul emerges
From dark confusion, now she knows the worst.
My sight is clear'd, my enterprise resolv'd,
And hope enlarges my advent'rous spirit.
    1 *Colc.* I hear in wonder, prince. At least prepare
       thee
To guard Medea in her new distress,
Whom Creon threatens to expel.
    Jas. The priestess will be her safeguard till . . . .
    1 *Colc.* Restrain thy speech,
And look behind thee. He is sent from Creon
To drive her hence.

Enter LYCANDER.

    Jas. Lycander!
    Lyc. Prince, allow me
With this old Colchian to confer a moment.
    1 *Colc.* Nay, speak aloud.
    Lyc. Thou know'st my errand, Colchian.
    1 *Colc.* Yes, if our princess willingly depart not,
Thou wilt by force remove her.
    Jas. Base and impious!
Now should these hands, which yok'd the brazen bulls,

Divide thy limbs, and hurl the mangled fragments
From yonder promontory's brow to feast
The scaly monsters in the flood below ;
It were a righteous sacrifice to justice :
But thou art brother to the good Theano.

Lyc. Whom thou dost wrong in me. By her consent,
And on Medea's promise to depart,
I came to guide her with respectful care
To Corinth's verge.   Compassion for this princess,
Dread of the king, and rev'rence for the goddess,
With all thy changes, prince, perplex my course ;
That through the maze of this eventful day
I ne'er shall tread securely.

Jas. Nay, Lycander,
If thou art blameless . . . . .

Lyc. Stop.   The king is here
To widen this confusion.

Enter CREON *and Attendants.*

Creon. [*entering.*] I am told,
That with a pensive mien he left the palace,
And join'd a Colchian of Medea's train.
Gods! he is here—disorder'd—with Lycander
And that old stranger—all in sullen silence
At my appearance—Jason—He replies not !
What are your consultations ? Speak, Lycander !

Lyc. My liege, I cannot, uninform'd like thee.

Creon. Then, as a king and father, I demand
Of thee, Thessalian hero, why, confus'd
At my approach, thy countenance is fall'n ?

Jas. At thy approach ? More formidable pow'rs
Could never awe this heart, which nought hath van-
      quish'd
But its own frailties.

  Creon. Visions !

  Jas. Hear with patience.
The tutelary deity of Corinth
Sits here in awful judgment. Virtue pleads,
And pity weeps before her. Thou and I
At this tribunal show our guilty heads.
Long have we slumber'd on the couch of folly ;
Let us awaken from the cheating dream,
Nor each rebuke the other for his weakness,
But acquiesce in Juno's just decree.
I must annul my contract with thy daughter,
And bid her now eternally farewell.

  Creon. Eternally farewell ? I dream—Lycander,
Is not Medea gone ?

  Lyc. My lord, the time . . . .

  Creon. Inactive traitor ! Go and seize that fiend !

  Jas. [*to Creon.*] Hold. Thou esteem'st me still the
      gentle Jason,
The pliant vassal of my father's will,
And thy ambition. I am chang'd—My heart
Is full of tumult—New-created rage,
Rage at myself, at Æson too, and thee,
Now ravages my bosom—Then be counsell'd,
Nor tempt the wild, ungovernable transports
Of one distemper'd with a foul assemblage
Of guilt, despair, and shame.

Creon. Presumptuous boy !
Do thy exploits by sorcery achiev'd,
Do thy rude trophies from barbarians won,
Exalt thy pride to brave a Grecian monarch ?
When now, from all inheritance expell'd
A needy exile, thou hast no support,
But from my throne, whose patronage is granted
To thy imploring father.

    Jas. I reject it,
And own no patron, but my sword and name.
Can I want aid, the Argonautic leader ?
While Hercules, while Telamon and Peleus,
While sacred Orpheus, and the twins of Leda,
Remain unconquer'd to assert my cause ?

    Why do I measure folly back to folly,
And here degrade my honours and renown
With boasts resembling thine ? Farewell for ever.

                          [Exit cum Colc.

    Creon. Ha! I perceive his purpose. Haste, collect

                        [To one of his attendants.
A faithful band; secure Medea's vessel.
Ye blackest demons of resentment, rise ;
March by my side, and brandish you my sceptre !

                      [To another of his attendants.
Thou shut the city-gates ! Let none depart
Without my licence ! I will hold him still,
And cast him prostrate at Creüsa's feet !

Enter THEANO.

    Thea. I heard thy threat'ning voice, O blindly fix'd
In disobedience to the queen of gods.

Creon. Dar'st thou, sole auth'ress of thy sov'reign's
    ills,

Confront his anger? First on thee, confed'rate

                         [*To* Lycander,

With this rebellious, shall my vengeance fall.

By thy design'd misconduct Jason twice

Hath seen Medea.

Lyc. Chance, or heav'n's appointment,

Not my contrivance . . . .

Creon. Seize and drag him hence ;

Low in a dungeon hide him; chain him down

In damps and darkness !

Lyc. Citizens of Corinth,

This place is holy ! In the name of Juno

I claim protection !

Thea. Universal rev'rence,

From your forefathers at the birth of Corinth,

Hath guarded still th' inviolable grove.

Creon. Do ye recoil, ye cowards ? Rebel, traitor,

I will assemble those shall force this refuge,

The seat of priestly craft to aid sedition ;

When thou in torture shalt atone thy crime !

Thea. Once more I warn thee to revere a goddess.

Creon. No, I revere a god, the god of thunders !

Jove, thou didst toil for empire ; so shall Creon,

And show the earth a pattern of thy sway !

For empire thou thy father didst dethrone,

Thy Titan kindred plunge in deepest hell.

The giant, lancing from his hundred hands

A hundred rocks to shake th' Olympian tow'rs

Thou didst with labour vanquish ! Shall these shades

Which awe the vulgar, shall the ready prey
To ev'ry firebrand, or the woodman's ax,
Obstruct a king? No, insolent revolters,
Soon shall you see me lift the bloody scourge
Of chastisement, unsheath the sword of havoc,
And vindicate my glory!   [*Exit cum suis.*

    Thea. Impious man!
Do thou consult thy safety.

    Lyc. Be not anxious.
The king's own rashness shall secure Lycander.
Though years may roll on years, ere we again
Shall meet in peace.

Enter JASON.

    Jas. Medea to thy temple
Is fled from all her virgins, who entreat
Thy kind permission to pursue her steps,
Where'er her frenzy leads!

    Thea. My help is ready.
And to thy guardian care I trust my brother,
Whom Creon threatens with immediate death.
Yet something whispers, something sure divine,
That other clouds, of black events will break,
Ere a new morning rise on troubled Corinth.
" And we, surviving each portentous storm,
" Derive a sad security from horror."   [*Exit.*

    Lyc. Whate'er this mystic language may import,
Prince, give attention.

    Jas. Speak.

F

Lyc. Thy only course
Is to embark from Corinth with Medea.

Jas. It was my secret and determin'd purpose.

Lyc. Nor yet a secret. Our suspicious tyrant,
If he could rule his discontented subjects,
Would stop thy passage. But thy just design
The public shall befriend, by me alarm'd
At Creon's threat to violate the grove.

Jas. Can I requite thee?

Lyc. Let me serve thee first;
Requite me after, as my wants may dictate.
Is not thy father yonder?

Jas. Let him come.
Go, and expect me shortly on the beach.   [*Ex.* Lyc.

Enter ÆSON.

Æs. What have I heard? Th' exasperated king—

Jas. Hath told the truth. His daughter I relinquish.

Æs. Off with this bridal pageantry, which mocks
With gay delusion my disastrous age.
Reach me again my sable; from thy hand
I will receive it: from thy barb'rous hand
Let dust be sprinkled on my joyless head.
Nay, rather turn invincible against me;
Lock in that nervous gripe these snowy hairs;
And to the hov'ring eagles on the beach
Cast my disfigur'd relics! Dost thou pause?
Think'st thou, that Jason's father will be seen
Decrepid, tott'ring with distress and years,
A vagabond, a suppliant for protection

Among the happier princes? No, my son,
Though not like thee the faulchion I can wield,
And mow my foes before me, I can die!

   Jas. Com'st thou with threat'nings? That tremen-
        dous goddess,
Whose piercing eye from yonder fane discerns
Guile in its naked shape through ev'ry garb,
And marks ingratitude for signal vengeance,
Knows that we merit both to die: yet, dying,
We could not expiate our unmatch'd offence.

   Æs. What unaccustom'd, terrifying sternness
Frowns on that aspect? Gentle have I known thee
From infancy to manhood, ne'er before
Have felt thee dreadful!

   Jas. Ever from thy fears
Wilt thou take counsel? Can the voice of pity,
Benevolence, and equity, convey
No admonition? O exalt thy thoughts
From this base earth, the mansion of deceit,
Of perjuries and crimes. " Erect thy visage to
" Themis' heav'n-thron'd patroness of justice.
" Invoke her aid, that strengthen'd thou mayst hear,"
Nor be confounded at thy son's resolves.
By no persuasion, artifice, or menace,
My now-reviving dignity of mind
From its own summit shall again descend.

   Æs. What would my Jason?

   Jas. Take the holy priestess;
Repair to Creon: with united counsels

Him first from impious violence dissuade:
And then——

    Æs. To whose protection must I fly?

    Jas. To mine. Abandon Corinth, and at Thebes,
Not three days march from these detested gates,
Expect my presence. Hercules is there;
My friend, my soldier. He with ev'ry hero,
Who once obey'd my standard, will again
League their auxiliar swords, and save Iolcos.
Let this suffice—If not—Persist no more.
Thy son is fix'd, immoveable as fate.   [*Thunder.*

    Æs. Thy mightier genius awes me! I submit!
We are all guilty—Juno so proclaims!
But, oh! amid these prodigies, my Jason,
Not one alarms me like the rude commotion,
Which shakes thy placid bosom! Be compos'd.
I will conduct Theano to the king.   [*Exit.*

    Jas. Look down, connubial goddess, and with hope
              [Jas. *turning towards the Temple.*
Let thy appeas'd divinity indulge
A hero off'ring at thy holy shrine
His spirit humbled with repentant sighs.

    You too attend, ye favourable gales,
And swiftly waft us to the kind embrace
Of our companion, Orpheus; who shall breathe
" His tuneful consolation in a strain
" Of grief composing energy to charm"
Distraction's rage, till new-born reason smile.
Then with her children, lovely as the mother,
Shall blooming Tempé on its flow'ry lap

Again receive her; " while Penéus' stream
" Blends with the flitting warblers on his banks
" His murm'ring cadence to delight her ear:"
And I once more along th' accustom'd vale
Shall, by the lustre of the silent moon,
Walk by her side attentive, while her tongue
Unfolds the pow'rs of heav'n's resplendent train
Of magic numbers, and mysterious spells,
And feasts with knowledge my enraptur'd soul. [*Exit.*

Enter Colchians.

" Sire of Æetes, god rever'd   [*Iambics.*
" By our forefathers on their sands
" Bleach'd by the Euxin's restless foam,
" Effulgent origin of day;
" Who with illimitable view,
" As from the amber-portall'd east
" Thy coursers fiery-man'd proceed,
" See'st the deep-bosom'd woes of men;
   " Whether plac'd in mildest climes,   [*Trochaics.*
   " Or beneath thy sultry wheels,
   " Whether freezing near the pole,
   " All the various race of care.
" Yet to thy sad paternal eye   [*Iambics.*
" Can this diversity of grief
" Not one present through all thy course
" To match thy own Medea's pain.
" Lo! ev'ry flow'r of wisdom fades
" Within her large and fertile breast,
" A desert now by tempests rang'd,

F iij

" The seat of wild discordant thoughts.
   " God of wisdom and of light,   [*Trochaics.*
   " O relume her darken'd soul !
   " Let her, though begirt with ills,
   " Still thy progeny be known.   [*Exeunt.*"

ACT V.   SCENE I.

THEANO *descending from the Temple,* ÆSON *and*
Colchians.

Æson.

WHERE is the priestess, Colchian ?
  1 *Colc.* There descending.
Pale consternation overcasts her visage.
  Thea. O most portentous, execrable sight !
I led the virgins to rejoin your princess,
Who had escap'd their care—Mysterious Heav'n !
Where was thy pow'r to check a mother's rage ?
Where was thy mercy, when her savage hand
Unclos'd the jaws of slaughter on her children ?
  Æs. Oh ! all-surpassing evil !
  1 *Colc.* When and how ?   Oh, speak !
  Thea. A knife of sacrifice she seiz'd,
And in their tender bosoms plung'd its point !
We found her planted near their welt'ring limbs ;
Her fiery eye-balls on their wounds were fix'd ;
A ghastly triumph swell'd her wild revenge,
And madness mingled smiles with horror !
  Æs. Horror

Is my companion now! The race of Jason
One common crime hath swallow'd in its gulph !

   Thea. The goddess bow'd in pity from her shrine ;
When straight a voice, oracular in thunder,
Whose awful clamour must have reach'd your ears,
Peal'd o'er the rocking temple. ' Impious Creon.'
The voice proclaim'd, ' thy guilt hath fill'd its mea-
        sure ;
' Then fall, thou victim to the gods of hell!'

   Æs. Tremendous sentence !

   Thea. I, with fearful steps,
Haste to the palace.

   Æs. Make me thy associate,
And I to calm his violence will join.

               [*Exeunt* Theano *and* Æson.

MEDEA *rushing from the Temple,* Phæacians *following.*

   1 *Colc.* Behold, where, dropping with her children's
      blood,
The lost Medea comes !

   Med. It is begun !
Now, to complete my vengeance, will I mount
The burning chariot of my bright forefather ;
The rapid steeds o'er Corinth will I drive,
And, with the scatter'd lightnings from their manes,
Consume its walls, its battlements and tow'rs,
Its princes, people, palaces, and temples !
Then, as the flames embrace the purple clouds,
And the proud city crumbles from its base,
The demon of my rage and indignation,

All grim and wrapt in terror, shall bestride
The mountainous embers, and denounce abroad
To gods and men my wrongs, and my revenge!

  1 *Colc.* How is thy wisdom exil'd from thy breast,
Its native seat, nor leaves one trace behind
To show it once was there!

  Med. Weep'st thou, old man?
Ha! speak; thou venerable mourner, speak
Thy cause of anguish! Hadst thou not a daughter
Wise like Minerva, like the morning fair,
And once thy dearest comfort? Hath she left thee,
Left thy decrepid head for grief to seize
And dash against the tomb? " Weep, weep, old man,
" The slight remainder of thy days exhaust
" In lamentation; she is lost for ever,
" Lost to herself and thee : and never more
" Shalt thou the beauty of her face contemplate,
" Nor hear again the wisdom of her tongue."

  1 *Colc.* Thou dost mistake me for thy stern Æetes.
I am but one among th' unnumber'd Colchians,
Who mourn in thee their nation's glory fall'n.

  Med. I well deserve this pity—yours—and yours,
Who kindly weep around me. As I pass,
I wade through seas of tears—I hear no sound
But sighs and groans from sorrow-beaten breasts.
Dishevell'd fragments of uprooted hairs
From the wild head of anguish fly about me!

  Is it not fitting? When Medea mourns,
Shall not the skies assume their blackest robes,
And scowl upon mankind? Medea sighs;

  2

Shall not hell groan, and heav'n reply in thunder?
It is the offspring of the Sun, who wrings
Her helpless hands, who rends her scatter'd locks!
    My heart is cold—The thread of life unwinds.
Now triumph, death—Thy conquest is Medea!

          [*She sinks into the lap of a* Phæacian.

    1 *Colc.* Repose her harass'd limbs with tend'rest
          care.

If this delirious transport be no more,
Than some short tumult of the heated brain;
Refreshing sleep may cool that seat of thought,
And wand'ring reason sojourn there again.

    Essay your vocal pow'r, harmonious maids;
Some new and soothing modulation choose;
Dress in persuasive melody your numbers,
Whose artful cadence from the breaking heart
May steal its cares, and fold them in oblivion.

          A Phæacian *turning towards the sea.*
Azure god, whose active waters   [*Trochaics.*
    Beat with endless toil below,
Calm the ruder blasts to slumber;
    While to yonder grove, which bends
Stately o'er thy shaded bosom,
    Softly-sighing gales aspire.
And, ye zephyrs, which ascending
    Fan the plumy verdure there,
Lulling whispers, drowsy murmurs
    Through the trembling foliage breathe
O'er the wakeful brow of sorrow
    Care beguiling sleep to spread.

Or my gently-soothing measure
 On your downy pinions bear
Through the grief-distemper'd spirit
 With delusion sweet to steal,
Till, on music's lap dissolving,
 Madness lull its weary head.

 1 *Colc.* Your queen recovers, and her look serene
Shows, the mild beam of reason shines anew.

 Med. Grief, as o'erlabour'd with its cruel office,
Awhile is pausing, till its strength return.
I will at least possess the short relief
To see my infants. Sure, my faithful friends,
From my sad heart no evils can erase
Maternal gladness at my children's sight.
Go, lead them from the temple—They will smile,
And lift my thoughts to momentary joy.

 Not gone, my virgins? Wherefore this delay?
Why all aghast? Why tremble thus your limbs?
Ha! whence this blood? My hands are dipt in
   slaughter.

Speak, ye dumb oracles of terror, speak! [*Rising.*
Where are my children? My distracted brain
A thousand dreadful images recalls
Imperfectly remember'd—Speak, I charge you?
Where are my children?—Silent still and pale!

 Enough—Fell pow'rs, your purpose is accomplish'd;
Medea's suff'rings are complete and full!

 1 *Colc.* The swelling passions struggle in her breast,
And find no vent. My ever-honour'd mistress,
This is the time for tears and exclamations.

Med. Can exclamations down the wind convey
From these retentive ears my children's groans ?
Or can this murd'rous hand by tears be whiten'd ?

" Hear, Neptune ! o'er this citadel emerge
" To reach my crime ; or send the pow'r of whirl-
          winds
" To sweep my footsteps from the stable earth !
" In rapid flight to Caucasus transport
" And fix me shiv'ring on the pointed rock !
" Let Nemesis revive the breathless clay
" Of my slain infants, to the rav'nous beak
" Their lips disfigure, and their tender fingers
" Arm with the vulture's talons ; that their wounds
" May be imprinted on their mother's breast
" With Promethèan torture, and her heart
" In blood bewail the error of her hand !"

1 *Colc.* It was the act of ignorance and madness.
Just Themis knows thy purity of mind,
And will, with pity, cleanse that erring hand.

Med. Not the disburthen'd sluices of the skies,
The wat'ry nereids with the ocean's store,
Nor all the tears, which misery hath shed,
Can from the mother wash her children's blood !

Where shall I hide me from the piercing day ?
What man will grant protection to my guilt,
What god afford me safeguard to his altar ?
Thou must alone receive me, thou, O earth !
Then, while I crush my bosom on thy surface,
And grasp the dust within my struggling hands,
Distain my limbs, and strike my head against thee,

At length in pity of my suff'rings sue
The loit'ring gods to rear the friendly bolt,
And close my sorrows on thy peaceful breast!
   1 *Colc.* See Jason too unconscious of his loss!

Enter JASON.

  Jas. Is she restor'd?
  1 *Colc.* Restor'd to full sensation
Of her increas'd afflictions, there she lies.
   Jas. " They shall be soon diminish'd! fate at last
" Hath folded up its inauspicious scroll,
" And fairer volumes open to our eyes.
" I see, you doubt me all. That pale dejection
" Reveals distrust and fear! I tell you, Colchians,
" Prophetic Themis from her spotless shrine,
" When she unfolds the oracle of justice,
" Fills not her priest with more enraptur'd fervor,
" Than now her present deity supplies
" To my stability of soul, which marks
" Success in prospect, and will show me still
" Not less than Jason in the brightest hour,
" Yourselves can witness, of his pass'd achievements."
Perhaps she sleeps!   [*Looking attentively on* Medea.
   1 *Colc.* Ah! no.
  Jas. Then, dearest woman,
Look on me, hear me, trust me once again.
I have resign'd Creüsa and her kingdom;
I have appeas'd my father; Creon's wrath
Is ineffectual now : then deign to cast
One glance on Jason, on thy suppliant husband

Return'd in tears of penitence and shame,
But with redoubled tenderness and truth!

Med. Oh! Jason—Thou and I have once been happy!
What are we now?

Jas. Let thy forgiving breath
Revive my courage fetter'd yet and tame
With thy displeasure; and my active love
Shall soon transport thee from this seat of wo;
Then, as we bound before the fav'ring gale,
Shall fondly whisper, we may still be happy!

Med. [*Starting up.*] Survey these hands!

Jas. What blood is this?

Med. Thy children's.

Jas. Inhuman Creon! could thy malice choose
No other victims than my blameless boys?
I come, incens'd Corinthians, to divulge
This profanation through your madding streets;
Myself will guide your torrent of revolt,
And whelm its billows on this royal savage!

Med. If heav'n had once meant kindly to Medea,
Some tyrant had been found, some other hand,
Than hers alone to spill her children's blood!

The season for upbraiding is no more;
But know, thou wretched like myself, that madness
Arm'd my blind rage against them, and the deed
Now weighs me down to everlasting night!

Jas. [*Falling on his knees.*] O thou, whose equal ba-
         lance to mankind
Distributes justice and restoring mercy,
If pray'rs from this polluted breast may reach

Thy pure abode, exert thy righteous pow'r;
Drop thy assuaging pity on her heart ;
On me exhaust the quiver of thy vengeance !

  Med. Was not my portion of distresses large
Ye pow'rs obdurate ? Hath this heart refus'd
To sigh, these eyes been sparing of their streams?
Impell'd by indignation, still my spirit
Would challenge your injustice, which requir'd
My children's blood to mingle with my tears.

  Take back the mighty mind you fram'd to break,
First rent by anguish, then by guilt deform'd!
                            [*Draws a poniard.*

  [*A voice from the temple.*] Hold, offspring of the Sun;
        arise ; repair
To Juno's shrine ; reply not, but obey.

    " Med. *Malignant goddess, to prolong my pain,*
" *Dost thou unbrace the firmness of my arm !*
                      " [She drops the dagger.

" *Yes, to accuse thee at thy shrine I come !—*
" *The guardian thou of marriage, hast permitted*
" *The violation of connubial faith ;*
" *And from that shrine didst pityless behold*
" *The fruit of marriage by a mother's hand*
" *Dash'd on thy pavement !*   [Thunder and lightning.
  " *Yes, amidst thy lightnings*
" *And triple bolted thunder shalt thou hear*
" *My execrations to provoke thy terrors ;*
" *Who, single auth'ress of Medea's wrongs,*
" *Dost now suspend the period of her woes.*   [Exit *Med.*"

  Jas. Celestial presence, I adore thy greatness ;

Yet thy tremendous voice, which rocks these bulwarks,
Appals not me, who bid destruction welcome!
Hope, which cements the structure of the heart,
From mine is moulder'd, and despair is lodg'd
Within the ruins.　　　　　　　　　[*He falls.*

Enter LYCANDER.

　Lyc. Gods! what new reverse
Hath cast the first of heroes to the earth?
Thy mariners expect thee; haste away.
Too high the ferment rises! Oh! recall
Theano's last presage of black events!
The wild impatience of religious rage
Stings ev'ry bosom!　" Our Corinthian dames
" Range through the streets with torches in their
　　　　hands,
" Invoking Juno, hymeneal Juno!
" An impulse more than natural directs
" Those armed numbers to some hideous act!
" They breathe demoniac fury on the palace!
" Should Creon meet them he must fall."　Rise,
　　　　prince;
I must attend thy flight.　Our timely absence
Will save our streets from homicide!
　Jas. No, death may reach me too!
　Lyc. For pity—Ha! the skies
Share in our tumult, and a bloody veil
Hangs o'er the sick'ning sun! The air wheels round us!
Grim Neptune yonder shakes his stormy trident!
　　　　　　　G ij

Why heaves the loosen'd rock? Why drop these
     clouds
In threat'ning murmurs from their dusky folds
Streak'd with sulphureous gleams?

       [*Thunder, lightning, and the stage darken'd.*
   Jas. [*rising.*] This suits my soul
For its infernal journey all prepar'd,
A pale attendant on my children's ghosts
In Tartarus to dwell, while they repose
In blest Elysium!

    1 *Colc.* Look, the holy priestess
Breaks from the palace in disorder'd haste,
And to her temple flies! In consternation
Old Æson too is nigh.

Enter ÆSON *and* Thessalians.

   Æs. My son! my son!
   Jas. If thou dost bring fresh evils thou art welcome!
   Æs. We found the harden'd king! My words were
     vain,
So were Theano's! With a desp'rate band,
Of life regardless, and contemning Juno,
Against her grove he sallies!

    Creon. [*behind the scenes.*] Since no longer
You dread my sceptre, you shall feel my sword;
" Which o'er your mangled carcases shall hew
" Its purple passage to chastise the author
" Of this revolt, and chase barbarians hence."

    Lyc. The king's rash voice. He charges.

              [*A shout within.*

Æs. Hideous roar !   [*Thunder and lightning.*
O Jove, be merciful !

Lyc. He gives the signal,
And shows the tumult through those livid flames !

Jas. I hear the clang of arms ! Unmov'd and cold,
My heart rejects that once-enliv'ning sound,
And sighs for dissolution ! Pause awhile,
Sad spirit, till Medea's fate is known,
Then prompt my sword to justice on myself !

Æs. That shout denounces triumph !

Lyc. Yes, and safety,
To all but Creon.   Give the torrent way !

Enter Corinthians.

1 *Cor.* Where is the honour'd priestess ?   We will
          bring,
If she so wills, the sacrilegious head
Of our slain tyrant to her sacred feet !

Lyc. Be silent all ! Theano from the goddess
To this assembly moves ! Night flies before her ;
Earth, seas, and heav'ns are calm'd !

Enter THEANO.

Thea. Ye sons of Corinth,
Old men of Colchis and Thessalians, hear !
At length the gods restrain their vengeful rod !
The dreadful scene is clos'd ! Iolchian prince,
Thou from Æetes' daughter art disjoin'd !
Look, where the goddess through th' aerial champain
Sends in a chariot, drawn by winged dragons,

That all-transcending woman into climes
Remote, but whither is from thee conceal'd!

> > > > > > > > > > > > [*Thunder.*

> > " *Enter* MEDEA *in a Chariot.*

  " Med. *Fine breathing couriers through the fields of air,*
" *Arrest your course obedient to this wand ;*
" *Ah ! what detains me longer in the sight*
" *Of hateful Corinth ? but on thee to cast*
" *A parting look, and some forgiving tears,*
" *Shed on thy errors, Jason—Oh, farewell!*
" *Constrain'd by Juno, and my parent gods,*
" *Who have subdu'd my anger, not my grief,*
" *O'er seas and earth to wander and explore*
" *The devious steps of destiny I go:*   [Thunder.
> > > > > > " [Exit in the chariot."

  Jas. Heav'n guide her fortunes. This shall govern
      mine. [*Offers to fall on his sword, but is prevented.*

  Thea. Unmanly desperation! Will the grave
Hide thy disgrace, or ill-tongu'd rumour die,
When thou art ashes? No. Recall thy manhood!
Thou hast a father's kingdom to redeem!
Go, save a nation! These afflicted maids,
These aged Colchians, to their homes restore.
Thus shall the censure, which thy frailty merits,
Be chang'd to blessings on thy gen'rous deeds,
And time's light finger loosen from thy breast
Its root of care, till peace of mind return!

> > > > > > > > > > [*Exeunt omnes.*

Hamilton. del.   Thornthwaite sculp.

Mrs. SIDDONS as CLEONE.

——— I hear his voice.

And this way he directs his hated Steps.

London Printed for J. Bell British Library Strand March 3 1792.

BRITTAIN.

CLEONE.

Cleone. Help! Mercy! Save!
Kill not my Infant——
Act V.

Hamilton pinxt.   A. Smith sculp

CLEONE.

A

TRAGEDY,

BY MR. R. DODSLEY.

ADAPTED FOR

THEATRICAL REPRESENTATION,

AS PERFORMED AT THE

THEATRE-ROYAL, IN COVENT-GARDEN.

REGULATED FROM THE PROMPT-BOOKS,

By Permission of the Managers.

" The lines distinguished by inverted Commas, are omitted in the Representation."

LONDON :

Printed for the Proprietors, under the Direction of
JOHN BELL, British Library, STRAND,
Bookseller to His Royal Highness the Prince of Wales.

M DCC XCII.

TO

THE RIGHT HONOURABLE
PHILIP DORMER STANHOPE,
EARL OF CHESTERFIELD.

MY LORD,

ENCOURAGED by the favourable opinion of many among the most ingenious of my friends, but particularly animated by your Lordship's approbation, I ventured to bring this Play on the Stage, even after it had been refused where I first intended it should appear. As the reception it met with from the Public hath amply justified your Lordship's sentiments concerning it, permit me to take this opportunity of presenting it to You, as an unfeigned testimony of the respect I bear for your Lordship's distinguished merit, and as a grateful, though unequal, return for the many favours, which it is my pride to own, I have received from your hands. For I do not mean, my Lord, in this address, to offend your delicacy by a needless panegyric upon Your character, which will be deliver'd down with admiration to latest posterity, but to do

*the highest honour to my own, by thus publishing to
the world, that I have not been thought unworthy the
favour and patronage of the Earl of Chesterfield.*

I am,

my Lord,

with great Respect,

your Lordship's

most obliged and

obedient humble Servant,

R. DODSLEY.

PREFACE
TO THE THIRD EDITION.

A<small>N</small> imperfect hint towards the Fable of the following Tragedy, was taken from the Legend of St. Genevieve written originally in French, and tranlated into English about an hundred years ago by Sir William Lower. The first sketch of it, consisting then of Three Acts only, was shewn to Mr. Pope two or three years before his death, who inform'd me that in his very early youth, he had attempted a Tragedy on the same subject, which he afterwards destroy'd ; and he advised me to extend my plan to Five Acts.

It lay by me, however, for some years, before I pursu'd it ; discourag'd by the apprehension of failing in the attempt : but happening at last to discover a method of altering and extending it, I resum'd my design; and as leisure from my other avocations permitted, have brought it to its present state.

I cannot omit this opportunity of repeating my acknowledgments to the Public for the continuance of their candid reception to these imperfect scenes. The Performers also are entitled to my thanks, for their diligent application to their respective parts, and for their just and forcible manner of representing them.

I have endeavoured in this third‡ edition to avail myself of every material objection that hath come to my knowledge, as far

‡ Printed in 1759.

B

as I could do so without totally altering the fable ; not indeed
with the vain hope of producing at last a faultless piece, but in
order to render it in fome degree less unworthy of that indulgence
with which it has been honour'd.   I have only to add, that if it
should be acted another season, I could wish it might be studied
from the present copy, as I hope it is not only more correct, but
somewhat improved.

CLEONE.

THIS Play, the production of one of the greatest protectors of letters in others, and a man of no mean powers himself, is built in part upon the old French legend of ST. GENEVIEVE.

DODSLEY offered it to GARRICK, but the manager declined it for a cause to him sufficient—it contained no character expressly suited to his own great powers.

To the other house, therefore, it was taken, and in 1758 acted with universal applause. Miss BEL-LAMY sustained the trying character of the principal, and in the conclusive scenes of maternal agony over her murdered child harrowed the hearts of the audience with powers then at their height, and by many conceived of the highest excellence.

The whole of this Drama is chastely written; with no aim after decorative pomp, or figurative anguish. NATURE presides over the whole, and dictates through a tender mind every sentiment of CLEONE.

The distress is perhaps too horrible for female minds to bear; — the maternal feelings are those which vibrate with the greatest keenness of sensation.

PROLOGUE.
By WILLIAM MELMOTH, Esq.

Spoken by Mr. ROSS.

'TWAS once the mode inglorious war to wage
With each bold bard that durst attempt the stage,
And Prologues were but preludes to engage.
Then mourn'd the Muse not story'd woes alone,
Condemn'd to weep, 'with tears unfeign'd, her own.
Past are those hostile days : aud wits no more •
One undistinguished fate with fools deplore.
No more the Muse laments her long-felt wrongs,
From the rude licence of tumultuous tongues :
In peace each bard prefers his doubtful claim,
And as he merits, meets, or misses, Fame.
'Twas thus in Greece (when Greece fair science blest,
And Heav'n-born arts their chosen land possest)
Th' assembled people sate with decent pride,
Patient to hear, and skilful to decide ;
Less forward far to censure than to praise,
Unwillingly refus'd the rival Bays.
Yes ; they whom candour and true taste inspire,
Blame not with half the passion they admire ;
Each little blemish with regret descry,
But mark the beauties with a raptur'd eye.
Yet modest fears invade our Author's breast,
With Attic lore, or Latian, all unblest ;

Deny'd by Fate through classic fields to stray,
Where bloom those wreaths which never know decay :
Where arts new force from kindred arts acquire,
And poets catch from poets genial fire.
Not thus he boasts the breast humane to prove,
And touch those springs which generous passions move,
To melt the soul by scenes of fabled wo,
And bid the tear for fancy'd sorrows flow ;
Far humbler paths he treads in quest of fame,
And trusts to Nature what from Nature came.

B iij

Dramatis Personae.

COVENT-GARDEN.

Men.

SIFROY, *a general officer*, - -	- Mr. Rofs.
BEAUFORT *senior, father of* Cleone, -	- Mr. Ridout.
BEAUFORT *junior, her brother*, -	- Mr. Dyer.
PAULET, *the friend of* Sifroy, -	— Mr. Clarke.
GLANVILLE, *a near relation*, -	- Mr. Sparks.
RAGOZIN, *a servant corrupted by* Glanville,	Mr. Anderson.

Women.

CLEONE, *the wife of* Sifroy, - -	- Mrs. Bellamy.
ISABELLA, *her companion*, - -	- Mrs. Elmy.
A CHILD *about five years old*.	

Officers of Juftice, Servants, &c.

SCENE, Sifroy's Houfe, and an adjoining Wood.

TIME, that of the Action.

CLEONE.

ACT I. SCENE I.

A Room in SIFROY'S *House. Enter* GLANVILLE *and*
ISABELLA.

Glanville.

WHAT means this diffidence, this idle fear?
Have I not given thee proof my heart is thine?
Proof that I mean to sanctify our joys
By sacred wedlock? Why then doubt my truth?
Why hesitate, why tremble thus to join
In deeds, which justice and my love to thee
Alone inspire? If we are one, our hopes,
Our views, our interests ought to be the same.
And canst thou tamely see this proud Sifroy
Triumphant lord it o'er my baffled rights?
Those late acquir'd demesnes, by partial hand
Consign'd to him, in equity are mine.

 Isab. The story oft I've heard: yet sure Sifroy
Hath every legal title to that wealth

By will bequeath'd ; and childless should he die,
The whole were thine.   Wait then till time—
    Glan. Art thou,
My Isabella, thou an advocate
For him whose hand, with felon-arts, with-holds
Those treasures which I covet but for thee ?
Where is thy plighted faith ?—thy vows ?—thy truth ?
    Isab. Forbear reproach !—O Glanville, love to thee
Hath robb'd me of my truth—seduc'd me on
From step to step, till virtue quite forsook me.
False if I am, 'tis to myself, not thee ;
Thou hast my heart, and thou shalt guide my will,
Obedient to thy wishes.
    Glan. Hear me then—
This curst Sifroy stands in my fortune's way ;
I must remove him.—Well I know his weakness—
His fiery temper favours my design,
And aids the plot that works his own undoing.
Yet whilst far off remov'd, he leads our troops,
The nation's doughty chief, he stands secure,
Beyond the reach of my avenging hand.
But this will force him home—I have convey'd,
By Ragozin his servant, whom I sent
On other business, letters which disclose
His wife's amour with Paulet.
    Isab. Ah ! tho' me
Thou hast convinc'd, and I believe her false,
Think'st thou Sifroy will credit the report ?
Will not remembrance of her seeming truth,

Her artful modesty, and acted fondness,
Secure the easy confidence of love?

   Glan. I know it ought not. Weak must be the man
Who builds his hopes on such deceitful ground.
Paulet is young, not destitute of passion;
Her husband absent, they are oft together:
Then she hath charms to warm the coldest breast,
Melt the most rigid virtue into love,
And tempt the firmest friendship to be frail.
All this I've urg'd, join'd with such circumstance,
Such strong presumptive proof, as cannot fail
To shake the firm foundations of his trust.
This once accomplish'd, his own violence
And heated rage, will urge him to commit
Some desperate act, and plunge him into ruin.

   Isab. But grant thou shouldst succeed, what will
       ensue?
Suppose him dead, doth he not leave an heir,
An infant son, that will prevent thy claim?

   Glan. That bar were easily remov'd.—But soft,
Who's here? 'Tis Ragozin return'd.

Enter RAGOZIN.

   Glan. What news,
Dear Ragozin? How did Sifroy receive
My letters? Speak—My vast impatience would
Know all at once.—What does his rage intend?

   Rag. All you could wish. A whirlwind is but weak
To the wild storm that agitates his breast.
At first indeed he doubted—swore 'twas false—

Impossible—But as he read, his looks
Grew fierce ; pale horror trembled on his cheek ;
O she is vile !—It must, it must be so—
Glanville is just, is good, and scorns to wrong her—
I know his friendship, know his honest heart—
Then falling, sobb'd in speechless agony.

    Glan. Good, very good !—I knew 'twould gall—
        proceed.

    Rag. His smother'd grief at length burst forth in
        rage.

He started from the floor —he drew his sword—
And fixing it with violence in my grasp—
Plunge this, he cry'd, O plunge it in the heart
Of that vile traitor, Paulet !—Yet forbear—
That exquisite revenge my own right hand
Demands, nor will I give it to another !
This said—push'd on by rage, he to her sire
Dispatch'd a letter, opening to him all
Her crime, and his dishonour.   This to you.

                          [Gives a letter.

    Glan. How eagerly he runs into the toils,
Which I have planted for his own destruction !—
Dear Ragozin, success shall double all
My promises ; and now we are embark'd,
We must proceed, whatever storms arise.

    Isab. But read the letter.

                *[Glanville *opens the letter and reads.*

  " Tho' thou hast stabb'd me to the heart, I cannot
" but thank thy goodness for the tender regard thou
" hast shewn to my honour. The traitor Paulet shall

" die by my own hand : that righteous vengeance must
" be mine. Mean time, forbid the villain's entrance
" to my house. As to her who was once my wife, let
" her go to her father's, to whom I have written ;
" leaving it to him to vindicate her virtue, or conceal
" her shame. I am in too much confusion to add more.
                                    " SIFROY."

This is enough—by Heaven! I sought no more.
It is the point at which my wishes aim'd.
The death of Paulet must include his own ;
Justice will take that life my injuries seek,
Nor shall suspicion cast one glance on me.
But does he purpose soon to leave the army,
Or let his vengeance sleep ?
    Rag. All wild he raves,
That honour should forbid to quit his charge.
Yet what resolves the tumult in his breast
May urge, is hard to say.
    Glan. We must prepare
For his arrival ; well I know his rage
Will burst all bounds of prudence. Thou, my friend,
(For from the hour which shall complete our business,
Thy servitude shall cease) be diligent
To watch all accidents, and well improve
Whatever chance may rise.
    Rag. Trust to my care.   [*Exit.*
    Glan. Now, Isabella ! now th' important hour
To prove my truth, arises to my wish.
No longer shalt thou live the humble friend

3

Of this Cleone, but, her equal born,
Shalt rise by me to grace an equal sphere.

Isab. Her equal born I am—nor can my heart
A keener pang than base dependence feel.
Yet weak by nature, and in fear for thee,
I tremble for th' event.—O shouldst thou fail—

Glan. To me,. my Isabella, trust the proof
Of her conceal'd amour. I know full well
Her modesty is mere disguise, assum'd
To cheat the world; but it deceives not me.
I shall unveil her latent wickedness,
And on her midnight revels pour the day.

Isab. Scarce can my heart give credit—

Glan. Thou, alas,
Art blinded by the semblance she displays
Of truth and innocence; but I explore
Her inmost soul, and in her secret thoughts
Read wantonness. Believe me, this gay youth,
Mask'd in the guise of friendship to Sifroy,
Is her vile paramour. But I forget;
Tell Ragozin, my love, to wait without;
This business asks dispatch, and I may want
His useful aid.

Isab. I go; but still my heart
Beats anxious, lest the truth of thy suspicions
Should fail of proof.   [*Exit* Isabella.

Glan. Fear nothing, I'm secure.—
Fond, easy fool! whom for my use alone,
Not pleasure, I've ensnar'd; thou little dream'st,
That fir'd with fair Cleone's heaven of charms,

I burn for their enjoyment. There, there too,
Did this Sifroy, this happy hated rival,
Defeat the first warm hopes that fir'd my bosom.
I mark'd her beauties rising in their bloom,
And purpos'd for myself the rip'ning sweetness;
But ere my hand could reach the tempting fruit,
'Twas ravish'd from its eager grasp. And, oh!
Would fate at last permit me to prevail,
Vengeance were satisfy'd. I will attend her;
And urge my suit, tho' oft repuls'd, once more.
If she's obdurate still, my slighted love
Converts to hatred: I will then exert
The power which her deluded lord hath given,
Drive her this instant hence, and in her flight,
To glut my great revenge, she too shall fall.   [*Exit.*

SCENE III.

Changes to another Room.   *Enter* CLEONE, *and a Servant.*

   Cle. Paulet! my husband's friend! give him admittance;
His friendship sympathizes with my love,
Cheers me by talking of my absent lord,
And sooths my heart with hopes of his return.

Enter PAULET.

   Pau. Still do these low'ring clouds of sorrow shade
Cleone's brow, and sadden all her hours?

   Cle. Ah Paulet! have I not just cause to mourn?

C

Three tedious years have past since these sad eyes
Beheld my dear Sifroy: and the stern brow
Of horrid war still frowns upon my hopes.

Pau. The fate of war, 'tis true, hath long detain'd
My noble friend from your fond arms and mine:
But his redoubted sword by this last stroke
Must soon reduce the foe to sue for peace.
The gallant chief who led the barbarous host,
And was himself their soul, is fallen in battle,
Slain by the valiant hand of your Sifroy.

Cle. To me, alas, his courage seems no virtue:
Dead to all joy, but what his safety gives,
To every hope, but that of his return,
I dread the danger which his valour seeks,
And tremble at his glory. O good Heaven!
Restore him soon to these unhappy arms,
Or much I fear, they'll never more enfold him.

Pau. What means Cleone? No new danger can
Affright you for my friend. I fear your breast
Beats with the dread of some impending ill,
Threatening yourself. Now, by the love that binds
My heart to your Sifroy, let me entreat,
If my assistance can avail you aught,
That, to the utmost hazard of my life,
You will command my service.

Cle. Kind Heaven, I thank thee! My Sifroy hath yet
One faithful friend. O Paulet—but to thee,
The many virtues that adorn the mind
Of my lov'd lord, and made me once so blest,
'Twere needless to display. In mine alone

His happiness was plac'd ; no grief, no care
Came ever near my bosom ; not a pain
But what his tenderness partaking, sooth'd.
All day with fondness would he gaze upon me,
And to my listening heart repeat such things,
As only love like his knew how to feel.
O my Sifroy! when, when wilt thou return ?
Alas, thou know'st not to what bold attempts
Thy unsuspecting virtue has betray'd me !

   Pau. What danger thus alarms Cleone's fear ?

   Cle. I am asham'd to think, and blush to say,
That in my husband's absence this poor form,
These eyes, or any feature should retain
The power to please—but Glanville well you know—

   Pau. Sure you suspect not him of base designs!
He wears the semblance of much worth and honour.

   Cle. So to the eye the speckled serpent wears
A shining beauteous form ; but deep within,
Foul stings and deadly poisons lurk unseen.
O Paulet, this smooth serpent hath so crept
Into the bosom of Sifroy, so wound
Himself about my love's unguarded heart,
That he believes him harmless as a dove.

   Pau. Good Heaven, if thou abhorr'st deceit, why
        suffer
A villain's face to wear the look of virtue ?
Who would have thought his loose desires had flown
So high a pitch ?—Have you imparted aught
Of his attempts to Isabella ?

   Cle. No.

C ij

Pau. I had suspicion his designs were there.

Cle. I've thought so too : nay have some cause to fear
That she's his wife. This hath restrain'd my tongue.

Pau. 'Tis well if she deserve your tenderness.
But say, Cleone, let me know the means,
Which this most impious man, this trusted friend,
Hath taken to betray—

Cle. I hear his voice ;
And this way he directs his hated steps.
Retire into that room—he seldom fails
To hint his bold desires. Your self perhaps
May thence detect him, and by open shame
Deter him from persisting. [Paulet *goes into the room.*

Enter GLANVILLE.

Glan. I greet you, lady, with important news ;
The Saracens are beaten—yet Sifroy,
Coldly neglectful of your blooming charms,
Pursues a remnant of the flying foe
To strong Avignon's walls, where shelter'd safe,
The hardy troops may bear a tedious siege.
Why then, Cleone, should you still resist
The soft entreaties of my warm desire ?
Methinks the man but ill deserves your truth,
Who leaves the sweet Elysium of your arms
To tread the dangerous fields of horrid war.

Cle. And what, O Glanville, what dost thou deserve ?
Thou, who with treachery repay'st the trust
Of sacred friendship ? Thou, who but to quench

A loose desire, a lawless passion's rage,
Would'st banish truth and honour from thy breast?

    Glan. Honour!—What's honour? A vain phantom rais'd
To fright the weak from tasting those delights,
Which Nature's voice, that law supreme, allows.
Be wise, and laugh at all its idle threats.
Besides, with me your fame would be secure,
Discretion guards my name from censure's tongue.

    Cle. And dost thou call hypocrisy, discretion?
Say'st thou that vice is wisdom? Glanville, hear me.
With thee, thou say'st, my fame would be secure;
Unsully'd by the world. It might. Yet know,
Tho' hid beneath the center of the earth,
Remov'd from envy's eye, and slander's tongue,
Nay from the view of Heaven itself conceal'd,
Still would I shun the very thought of guilt,
Nor wound my secret conscience with reproach.

    Glan. Romantic all! Come, come, why were you form'd
So tempting fair; why grac'd with ev'ry charm,
With eyes that languish, limbs that move with grace—
Why were these beauties given you, but to soothe
The sweet, the strong sensations they excite?
Why were you made so beauteous, yet so coy?

    [*Offers to embrace her, she puts him by with disdain.*
    Cle. Base hypocrite! why rather wert thou suffer'd
Beneath fair virtue's mien to hide a heart
So vile? Why this, good Heaven! But dost thou think
Thy foul devices shall be still conceal'd?

C iij

Sifroy shall know thee ; thy detested crime
Shall stand reveal'd in all its horrid form.

 Glan. Is love a crime ? O ask your feeling heart—
        [Paulet *bursts from the room.*

 Pau. Villain, desist !

 Glan. Ha ! Paulet here !—'Tis well :
He is her minion then ! 'Tis as I guess'd ;
My letters to Sifroy traduc'd them not.   [*Aside.*

 Pau. Vile hypocrite !—what ! lurk such warm desires
Beneath that sober mask of sanctity ?
Is this the firm undoubted honesty,
In which Sifroy confiding, sleeps secure ?

 Glan. And is it fit that thou should'st lecture vice ?
Thou who, even here, this moment wert conceal'd,
The favorite object of lewd privacy ?
Should'st thou declaim against the rich repast,
Thy gluttonous appetite alone enjoys
To all the heights of luxury ?—Sweet lady !
Who now shall stand reveal'd before Sifroy ?
But I have long, long known your intercourse,
Nor wanted clearer proof to speak your crimes.

          [*Going.*

 Cle. O heaven and earth !

 Pau. Stay, monster ! by high Heaven,
Thy life shall answer this vile calumny.

 Glan. Dream not I fear !—thy threatenings I despise.
Soon I'll return, to thine and her confusion.

        [*Exit* Glanville.

 Cle. What have I done ? unhappy rash concealment !
This may, alas ! give colour to his charge.

Pau. He dares not wrong you with the least sur-
      mise,
The slightest imputation on your fame !
Nor would the world believe him.   Your fair deeds,
The constant tenor of your virtuous life,
Would triumph o'er th' audacious tale.

  Cle. Ah, Paulet !
The sting of slander strikes her venom deep.
An envious world with joy devours the tale,
That stains with infamy a spotless name.
Yet what's the vain opinion of the world !
To keep one voice, one single heart's esteem,
Is all my wish.   If my Sifroy but think——

    Pau. Wound not your peace with vain ungrounded
      fears.
My friend is noble, knows your virtues well ;
Nor will he suffer jealousy to shake
His generous mind with doubt. And for that wretch,
This arm shall give him chastisement.

  Cle. Ah ! no ;
I fear the chastisement of Glanville's guilt
May loose the tongue of censure on my innocence.
And can I bear, now, in my husband's absence,
The whisper'd falsehood of malicious tales,
That cast a doubt on his Cleone's truth ?
O rather leave his punishment to Heaven !
At least defer it till my lord's return.

    Pau. And shall the man I love return, and find
A villain unchastis'd, who in my sight

Presumptuous dar'd to wound his honour!
It must not, shall not be.

Re-enter GLANVILLE *with* RAGOZIN.

Glan. Mark me, young Sir,
'Tis with authority that I forbid
Your entrance in this house.   Sifroy, convinc'd
Of all your secret crimes with that vile wanton,
Spurns from his door the falsehood he disdains.

 Cle. Let me not hear it! I! am I a wanton?
Does my dear lord think his Cleone vile?

 Glan. He knows it well.

 Pau. Villain, 'tis false! He scorns
So mean a thought.

 Glan. To silence every doubt,
See his own hand.

 Pau. [*Shewing the letter to* Ragozin.] Say, whence is
   this? who brought it?

 Rag. I brought it from my master.

 Glan. Look upon it.

[Cleone and Paulet look over it.

 Cle. Am I then banish'd from my husband's house?
Branded with infamy!—was once his wife!
Unkind Sifroy! am I not still thy wife?
Indeed thy faithful wife! and when thou know'st,
As know thou wilt, how falsely I'm accus'd,
This cruel sentence sure will pierce thy heart.

 Pau. Amazement strikes me dumb!—This impious
   scroll
Is forg'd.   Sifroy, tho' rash, is noble, just,

And good. Too good, too noble to permit
So mean a thought to harbour in his breast.

Cle. No : 'tis his hand—his seal. And can I bear
Suspicion ! Ah ! Sifroy, didst thou not know
My heart incapable——

Pau. Licentious wretch !
At what fell mischief has thy malice aim'd ?

Glan. At thine and her detection, which at length
I have accomplish'd.

Pau. Impudent and vain !
Think'st thou Cleone's virtue, her fair truth,
Can suffer taint from thy unhallow'd breath ?
Were they not proof but now against thy arts ?

Glan. Mistaken man ! To gain one personal proof
Of her incontinence, that feign'd attempt
Was made ; all other proof I had before.
And why I fail'd thou know'st ;
Who in her private chamber close conceal'd,
Mad'st it imprudent she should then comply.

Cle. Detested slanderer ! I despise thy baseness ;
Disdain reply ; and trust in Heaven's high hand
To dash thy bold designs.   [*Exit* Cleone.

Pau. [*Whispering.*] Observe me, Sir—
This insult on the honour of my friend
Must be chastis'd. At morning's earliest dawn,
In the close vale, behind the castle's wall,
Prepare to meet me arm'd.

Glan. Be well assur'd
I will not fail.   [*Exit* Paulet.
Yet stay—let Prudence guide me——

Courage, what is't ?—'tis folly's boisterous rashness,
And draws its owner into hourly dangers.
I hold it safer he were met to-night.   [*Aside.*
Thou see'st, my Ragozin, we are embark'd
Upon a troubled sea : our safeties now
Depend on boldly stemming every wave,
That might o'erwhelm our hopes. Paulet must die—
He's dangerous, and not only may defeat
Our enterprise, but bring our lives in hazard.

  Rag. Shall we not frustrate thus your first design,
To make the law subservient to your aims
Against the life and fortunes of Sifroy ?

  Glan. Leave that to me. Sifroy, full well I know,
Will soon arrive. Thou, when the gloom of night
Shall cast a veil upon the deeds of men,
Trace Paulet's steps, and in his bosom plunge
Thy dagger's point : thus shall thy care prevent
His future babbling ; and to prove the deed
Upon Sifroy, be mine.

  Rag. He dies this night.

  Glan. Let thy first blow make sure his death,
So shall no noise detect thee. Hither strait
Convey his corpse, which secretly interr'd
Within the garden's bound, prevents discovery,
'Till I shall spring the mine of their destruction.

  Rag. He shall not live an hour.   [*Exit* Ragozin.

  Glan. Hence, hence remorse !
I must not, will not feel thy scorpion sting.
Yet hell is in my breast, and all its fiends
Distract my resolutions.—I am plung'd

In blood, and must wade thro': no safety now
But on the farther shore. Come then, revenge,
Ambition come, and disappointed love;
Be you my dread companions: steel, O steel
My heart with triple firmness, nerve my arm
With tenfold strength, and guide it to achieve
The deeds of terror which yourselves inspir'd.

ACT II. SCENE I.

A Room in SIFROY's *House.*   GLANVILLE *and*
ISABELLA.

Glanville.

SURE the dark hand of death ere this hath clos'd
The prying eyes of Paulet, and secur'd
Our bold attempt from danger. But hast thou,
Free from suspicion, to Cleone's hand
Convey'd the letter, forg'd against myself,
Pressing her instant flight, and branding me
With black designs against her life?

    Isab. I have;
Pretending 'twas receiv'd from hands unknown.
But lurks no danger here! Will not this letter,
Discover'd after death, thy guilt betray?

    Glan. There am I guarded too. The deed once done,
A deep enormous cavern in the wood
Receives her body, and for ever hides.
But she perus'd, thou say'st, the letter—Well—

How wrought it?—Say—this moment will she fly?
Success in this, and all shall be our own.

Isab. Silent she paus'd—and read it o'er and o'er.
Then lifting up her eyes—Forgive him, Heaven!
Was all she said.   But soon her rising fear
Resolv'd on quick escape.   Suspicion too,
That all her servants are by thee corrupted,
Prompts her to fly alone, save with her child,
The young Sifroy, whom clasping to her breast,
And bathing with a flood of tears, she means,
Safe from thy snares, to shelter with her father.

Glan. Just as I hop'd—Beneath the friendly gloom
Of Baden wood, whose unfrequented shades
They needs must pass to reach her father's house,
I have contriv'd, and now ordain their fall.
Kindly she plans her scheme, as tho' herself
Were my accomplice.

Isab. As we parted, tears
Gush'd from her eyes—she closely press'd my hand,
And hesitating cry'd—O Isabella!
If 'tis not now too late, beware of Glanville.
I scarce could hold from weeping.

Glan. Fool! root out
That weakness, which unfits th' aspiring soul
For great designs.   But hush! who's here?

Enter RAGOZIN.

Glan. Say, quickly—
Is our first work achiev'd?
Rag. Successfully.

With two bold ruffians, whose assisting hands
Were hir'd to make the business sure, I trac'd
His steps with care; and in the darksome path
Which leads beside the ruin'd abby's wall,
With furious onset suddenly attack'd him.
Instant he drew, and in my arm oblique
Fix'd a slight wound; but my associates soon
Perform'd their office; and betwixt them borne,
I left him to an hasty burial, where
Your first directed.

   Glan. We are then secure
From his detection; and may now advance
With greater safety. O my Ragozin,
But one step more remains, to plant our feet
On this Sifroy's possessions; and methinks
Kind opportunity now points the path
Which leads us to our wish.

   Rag. Propose the means.

   Glan. This hour Cleone with her infant boy,
Borrowing faint courage from the moon's pale beam,
Prepares to seek the mansion of her father.
Thou know'st the neighbouring wood through which
       they pass.

   Rag. I know each path and every brake.

   Glan. There hid
In secret ambush, thou must intercept
Her journey.

   Rag. And direct her to the world
Unknown.

   Glan. Thou read'st my meaning right. Go thou

D

To hasten her departure, and to keep   [*To* Isabella.
Her fears awake.

   Isab. Already she believes
Her life depends upon her instant flight.

                            [*Exit* Isabella.

   Glan. And haply ours. Each moment that she lives
Grows dangerous now ; and should she reach her
         father,
All may be lost. Let therefore no delay
Hang on thy foot-steps : terror wings her flight :
Our danger calls at least for equal speed.

   Rag. They 'scape me not. I know the private path
They needs must tread thro' Baden's lonesome wood,
And death shall meet them in the dreary gloom.

   Glan. Meantime, soon as she leaves her house, I raise,
From whispering tongues, a probable report,
That she with Paulet seeks some foreign shore.
This will confirm her guilt, and shelter us
From all suspicion.

   Rag. True ; both gone at once
Will give an air of truth so plausible——

   Glan. Hark ! hush !

   Rag. Who is it ?

   Glan. 'Tis Cleone's voice !
This way she comes—we must not now be seen.
Fly to thy post, and think on thy reward.   [*Exeunt.*

         Enter CLEONE *with her Child.*

   Cle. No Paulet to be found ! Misfortune sure
Prevents his friendship ; and I dare not wait

For his assistance.   Friendless and alone
I wander forth, Heaven my sole guide, and truth
My sole support.   But come, my little love,
Thou wilt not leave me.

    Child. No, indeed I won't!
I'll love you, and go with you every where,
If you will let me.

    Cle. My sweet innocent!
Thou shalt go with me.   I've no comfort left
But thee.   I had—I had a husband once,
And thou a father.—But we're now cast out
From his protection, banish'd from his love.

    Child. Why won't he love us? Sure I've heard you
       say,
You lov'd him dearly.

    Cle. O my bursting heart!
His innocence will kill me. So I do,
My angel, and I hope you'll love him too.

    Child. Yes, so I will, if he'll love you : and can't
I make him love you?

    Cle. Yes, my dear ; for how
Could he withstand that sweet persuasive look
Of infant innocence!

    Child. O then he shall,
If ever I do see him, he shall love you.

    Cle. My best, my only friend! and wilt thou plead
Thy poor wrong'd mother's cause?

D ij

Enter ISABELLA.

Isab. Dear Madam, haste! why thus delay your
      flight,
When dangers rise around?

  Cle. Indeed, my steps
Will linger, Isabella.—O 'tis hard—
Alas, thou canst not tell how hard it is——
To leave a husband's house so dearly lov'd!
Yet go I must—my life is here unsafe.
Pardon, good Heaven, the guilt of those who seek it!
I fear not death: yet fain methinks would live
To clear my truth to my unkind Sifroy.

  Isab. O doubt not, Madam, he will find the truth,
And banish from his breast this strange suspicion.
But haste, dear lady, wing your steps with haste,
Lest death should intercept——

  Cle. And must I go?
Adieu, dear mansion of my happiest years!
Adieu, sweet shades! each well-known bower, adieu!
Where I have hung whole days upon his words,
And never thought the tender moments long——
All, all my hopes of future peace, farewell!
                [*Throws herself on her knees.*
But, O great Power! who bending from thy throne
Look'st down with pitying eyes on erring man,
Whom weakness blinds, and passions lead astray,
Impute not to Sifroy this cruel wrong!
O heal his bosom, wounded by the darts
Of lying slander, and restore to him

That peace, which I must never more regain. [*Rises.*
Come, my dear love, Heaven will, I trust, protect
And guide our wandering steps! Yet stay—who knows,
Perhaps my father too, if slander's voice
Hath reach'd his ear, may chide me from his door,
Or spurn me from his feet!—My sickening heart
Dies in me at that thought! Yet surely he
Will hear me speak! A parent sure, will not
Reject his child unheard!

 Isab. He surely will not. Whence these groundless
   fears?

 Cle. Indeed I am to blame, to doubt his goodness.
Farewell, my friend!—And oh, when thou shalt see
My still belov'd Sifroy; say, I forgive him—
Say I but live to clear my truth to him;
Then hope to lay my sorrows in the grave,
And that my wrongs, lest they should wound his peace,
May be forgotten.   [*Exit* Cleone, *with her Child.*

 Isab. Gracious Heaven! her grief
Strikes thro' my heart! Her truth, her innocence
Are surely wrong'd.—O wherefore did I yield
My virtue to this man? Unhappy hour!
But 'tis too late!—Nor dare I now relent.

Enter GLANVILLE.

 Glan. The gate is clos'd against her, never more
(If right I read her doom) to give her entrance.
Thus far, my Isabella, our designs
Glide smoothly on. The hand of prudence is
To me the hand of Providence.

Isab. Alas!

How blind, how impotent is human prudence!
I wish, and hope indeed, that screen'd beneath
The shades of night, which hide these darker deeds,
We too may lie conceal'd : but ah, my hopes
Are dash'd with fear, lest Heaven's all-piercing eye,
That marks our covert guilt, should flash detection.

    Glan. [*Sternly.*] If thy vain fears betray us not,
       we're safe.

Observe me well.—Had I the least surmise,
That struck by conscience, or by phantoms awed,
Thou now would'st shrink--and leave me, or betray--
By all the terrors that would shake my soul
To perpetrate the deed, thou too should'st fall!

    Isab. And canst thou then suspect, that after all
I've done to prove my love, I should betray thee?
O Glanville! thou art yet, it seems, to learn,
That in her fears tho' weak, a woman's love
Inspires her soul to dare beyond her sex.

    Glan. Forgive me, Isabella, I suspect
Thee not; this raging fever in my brain
Distracts my reason. But no more—I know
Thee faithful, and will hence be calm.

    Isab. Indeed my heart has been so wholly thine,
That ev'n its springs are temper'd to thy wish.

    Glan. Think on my warmth no more. I was to
       blame.

But come, my love, our chief, our earliest care
Must be to give loud rumour instant voice,
That both detected in their loose amour

Are fled together. Whisper thou the tale
First to the servants, in whose listening ears
Suspicions are already sown ; while I
Th' unwelcome tidings to her sire convey.

> [*Exit* Isabella *one way, and as* Glanville *is
> going out the other, he meets a Servant.*

Serv. My lady's brother, Sir, young Beaufort, just
Arriv'd, enquires for you, or for his sister.

Glan. Attend him in.—The letters of Sifroy
Have reach'd their hands. My story of her flight
Will, like a closing witness well prepar'd,
Confirm her guilt.

Enter BEAUFORT *junior.*

Beauf. jun. What strange suspicion, Glanville, has
            possess'd
The bosom of Sifroy ? Whence had it birth ?
Or on what ground could malice fix her stand,
To throw the darts of slander on a name
So guarded as Cleone's ?

Glan. I could wish——
It gives me pain to speak—but I could wish
The conduct of Cleone had not given
So fair a mark.

Beauf. jun. So fair a mark !—What ! who ?
Cleone, say'st thou !—Hath my sister given
So fair a mark to slander ?—Have a care !
The breath that blasts her fame may raise a storm
Not easily appeas'd.

Glan. It grieves me, Sir,
That you compel me to disclose, what you

In bitterness of soul must hear. But she
And prudence have of late been much estrang'd.

   Beauf. jun. Defame her not—Discretion crowns
        her brow,
And in her modest eye sweet innocence
Smiles on detraction.   Where, where is my sister?
She shall confront thy words—her look alone
Shall prove her truth, and calumny confound.

   Glan. You surely know not, Sir, that she is fled—
   Beauf. jun. What say'st thou? Fled!—Surprise
       choaks up my words!
It cannot be! Fled! whither?—Gone! with whom?
   Glan. With Paulet, Sir, Sifroy's young friend.
   Beauf. jun. Impossible!
I'm on the rack! Tell, I conjure thee, tell
The whole mysterious tale.   Where are they gone?

   Glan. That they conceal.   I only know, that both,
Soon as they found their impious love disclos'd,
With instant speed withdrew: and 'tis suppos'd
Will seek for shelter on some foreign shore.

   Beauf. jun. Where then is truth, and where is
        virtue fled,
Ere while her dear companions?—How, my sister,
How art thou fallen!—Thy father too—O parricide!
Had'st thou no pity on his bending age?
On his fond heart?—too feeble now to bear
So rude a shock.

   Glan. Can it not be conceal'd?
   Beauf. jun. That hope were vain.   Himself impa-
       tient comes,

From his lov'd daughter to enquire the cause
Of this opprobrious charge. And see, he's here.

Enter BEAUFORT *senior.*

   Beauf. sen. Where is my daughter ? where my in-
       jur'd child ?
O bring me to her! she hath yet a father,
(Thanks to the gracious powers who spar'd my life
For her protection) ready to receive
With tender arms his child, tho' rudely cast
From her rash husband's door. What mean these
       tears
That trickle down thy cheek ? she is not dead !
   Beauf. jun. Good Heaven ! what shall I say ?—No,
       sir—not dead—
She is not dead——but oh !——
   Beauf. sen. But what ? Wound not
My heart ! where is she ? lead me to my child—
'Tis from herself alone that I will hear
The story of her wrongs.
   Beauf. jun. Alas! dear Sir,
She is not here.
   Beauf. sen. Not here !
   Beauf. jun. O fortify
Your heart, my dearest father, to support,
If possible, this unexpected stroke !
My sister, Sir—why must I speak her shame !
My wretched sister, yielding to the lure
Of Paulet's arts, hath left her husband's house.

Beauf. sen. Great Pow'r! then have I liv'd, alas!
  too long.
This is indeed too much.   I cannot bear—
But 'tis impossible!—does not thy heart,
My son, bear testimony for thy sister
Against this calumny ?—What circumstance,

        [*To* Glanville.

What proof have we of my Cleone's guilt ?
 Glan. Is not their disappearing both at once,
A strong presumption of their mutual guilt ?
  Beauf. sen. Presumption, say'st thou! Shall one
   doubtful fact
Arraign a life of innocence unblam'd ?
Shall I give up the virtue of my child,
My heart's sweet peace, the comfort of my age,
On weak surmises ?—Sir, I must have proof,
Clear, unambiguous proof, not dark presumption.
 Glan. Thus rudely urg'd, my honour bids me speak,
What else I meant in tenderness to spare.
Know then, I found the wanton youth conceal'd
In her apartments.
  Beauf. sen. Thou dost then confess
Thyself my child's accuser ?—but thy word
Will not suffice: Far other evidence
Must force me to believe, that truth long known,
And native modesty, could thus at once
Desert their station in Cleone's breast.
 Glan. Wait then for other evidence—
With such as doubt my honour, I disdain
All further conference.   [*Exit* Glanville.

Beauf. jun. What can we think ?
His firm undaunted boldness fills my breast
With racking doubts, that dread to be resolv'd,
Yet this suspense is torture's keenest pang.

    Beauf. sen. We must not bear it. No, my son, lead
        on ;
We must be satisfy'd. Let us direct
Our steps to Paulet's habitation. There,
It seems, we must enquire. And yet my soul
Strongly impels me to suspect this Glanville ;
For can Cleone, virtue's fav'rite ward,
Thus totally be chang'd ?—If thou art fall'n—
If thy weak steps, by this bad world seduc'd,
Have devious turn'd into the paths of shame,
Never, ah ! never let me live to hear
Thy foul dishonour mention'd. If thou art
Traduc'd—and my fond heart still flatters me
With hope—then gracious Heaven ! spare yet my life,
O spare a father to redress his child !

ACT III. SCENE I.

The Area before SIFROY's *House.* SIFROY *alone.*

Sifroy.

O DREADFUL change ! my house, my sacred home,
At sight of which my heart was wont to bound
With rapture, I now tremble to approach.

Fair mansion, where bright honour long hath dwelt
With my renown'd progenitors, how, how
At last hath vile pollution stain'd thy walls!
Yet look not down with scorn, ye shades rever'd,
On your dishonour'd son—He will not die
Till just revenge hath by the wanton's blood
Aton'd for this disgrace.   Yet can it be?
Can my Cleone, she whose tender smile
Fed my fond heart with hourly rapture, she
On whose fair faith alone I built all hope
Of happiness—can she have kill'd my peace,
My honour? Could that angel form, which seem'd
The shrine of purity and truth, become
The seat of wantonness and perfidy?
Ye powers!—should she be wrong'd—in my own heart
How sharp a dagger hath my frenzy plung'd!
O passion-govern'd slave! what hast thou done?
Hath not thy madness from her house, unheard,
Driven out thy bosom friend?—Guiltless, perhaps—
Hell, hell is in that thought!—Thou wretch accurst,
Such thy rash fury, thy unbridled rage,
Her guilt or innocence alike to thee
Must bring distraɛtion.   But I'll know the worst.
                                             [*Exit.*

SCENE II.

Changes to a Room in the House.   GLANVILLE *and*
ISABELLA.

Glan. What dost thou say ? Already is Sifroy
Arriv'd ? Who saw him ? when ?

Isab. This moment, from
My window, by the glimmering of the moon,
I saw him pass.

Glan. He comes as I could wish.
His hot-brain'd fury well did I foresee
Would, on the wings of vengeance, swiftly urge
His homeward flight. But I am ready arm'd,
Rash fool ! for thy destruction. And tho' long
Thou hast usurp'd my rights, thy death at last
Shall give me ample justice.

Isab. Ah, beware ;
Nor seek his life at peril of thine own.

Glan. Trust me, my love, (tho' time too precious now
Permits not to unfold to thee my scheme)
I walk in safety, yet have in my grasp,
Secure, his hated life.—But see, he comes—
Retire.   [*Exit* Isabella.

Enter SIFROY.

Glan. [*Advancing to embrace him.*] My honoured
      friend !—

Sif. Glanville, forbear—
And ere I join my arms with thee in friendship,

E

Say, I conjure thee, by that sacred tie,
By all thou hold'st most dear on earth, by all
Thy hopes of heaven, and dread of deepest hell—
Hast thou not wrong'd my wife?

   Glan. Unjust Sifroy!
Hath my warm friendship thus regardful been,
Thus jealous of thy honour, and dost thou
Yet question mine? Sure the united bonds
Of friendship and of blood, are ties too strong
To leave a doubt of my sincerity.
And soon too clearly, Sir, you will discern
Who has been false, and who your faithful friend.

   Sif. O rack me not! let dread conviction come—
Her strongest horrors cannot rend my heart
With half the anguish of this torturing doubt.
Speak then—for tho' the tale should fire my brain
To madness, I must hear. Yet, Glanville, stay—
Let me proceed with caution—my soul's peace
Depends on this event. 'Tis said I am rash—
Bear witness! am I so?—Where is my wife?
Severe I may be, but I will be just.
I cannot, will not hear her faith arraign'd,
Before I see her.

   Glan. See her, Sir! alas,
Where will you see her?

   Sif. Where? thou hast not yet
Convey'd her to her father?—On the wings
Of speed I flew, still hoping to prevent
The rash decree of unreflecting rage.

Glan. Heaven give thee patience!—O Sifroy! my
       heart,
Tho' thou hast wrong'd it with unkind suspicion,
Bleeds for thy injuries, for thy distress.
The wife, whom thou so tenderly hast lov'd,
Is fled with Paulet.

Sif. Fled!—How? whither? when?

Glan. This day they disappear'd, and 'tis believ'd
Intend to fly from shame, and leave the land.

Sif. Impossible!—she cannot be so chang'd—
Was she not all my heart could wish?—Take heed—
Once more I charge thee, Glanville, and my soul's
Eternal welfare rests upon thy truth—
Traduce her not! nor drive me to perdition!
For by the flames of vengeance, if I find
Thy accusation true, they shall not 'scape!
Yes, I will trace th' adulterer's private haunts,
Rush like his evil genius on their shame,
And stab the traitor in her faithless arms—
Almighty Power! whose piercing eye explores
The depths of falsehood! take not from my arm
This due revenge—nor tempt mankind to doubt
The justice of thy ways. Why this intrusion?

Enter a Servant.

Serv. My lady's father, Sir.

Sif. Her father here!

Glan. Yes, he was here before—thy letters brought
       him,
And hence went forth in haste to find out Paulet.

Sif. Conduct him in.   [*Exit Servant.*
Unhappy man! his grief,
His venerable tears will wring my heart.
Retire, good Glanville; interviews like these,
Of deep-felt mutual wo, all witness shun.

                                        [*Exit* Glanville.

Enter BEAUFORT *Senior.*

Beauf. sen. Rash man! what hast thou done?—on
        what surmise
Dost thou impeach the honour of my name,
Sacred thro' many an age from ev'ry stain?
O! thou hast from thy bosom cast away
The sweetest flower that ever nature form'd.

Sif. Reproach me not—commiserate a wretch
On whom affliction lays her iron hand!
That flower, which look'd so beauteous to the sense,
Ran wild, grew ranker than a common weed.

Beauf. sen. It is not—cannot be! Have I not known,
Even from her earliest childhood known her heart?
Known it the seat of tenderness and truth?
Her thoughts were ever pure as virgin snows
From heaven descending: and that modest blush,
Display'd on her fair cheek, was virtue's guard.
She could not fall thus low—my child is wrong'd!
Ask thine own heart—recall her blameless life,
Was she not all a parent's fondest wish—

Sif. Call not to my distracted mind how good,
How bright she once appear'd. Time was indeed,
When blest in her chaste love, I fondly thought

My soul possess'd of all that earth held fair
And amiable : but memory of past bliss
Augments the bitter pangs of present wo!
Is she not chang'd—fallen—lost ?

   Beauf. sen. Patience, my son,
Compose the tempest of thy grief.   Just heaven
Will doubtless soon reveal the hidden deeds
Of guilt and shame.   If thy unhappy wife
Thus wanton in the paths of vice hath stray'd—
I would not rashly curse my darling child—
Yet hear me, righteous Heaven! May infamy,
Disease, and beggary imbitter all
Her wretched life! But my undoubting heart,
In full conviction of her spotless truth,
Acquits her of all crime.

   Sif. Is it no crime,
That listening to a vile seducer's voice,
She leaves her husband's house—her dearest friends?
Flies with her paramour to foreign climes,
A willing exile? Damn'd adult'ress! What,
Are these no crimes?

   Beauf. sen. Suppress thy rage.   They are :
But is she guilty? Art thou well inform'd
They went together? How doth it appear?
Who saw them? Where? Alas! thy headlong rage
Was too impatient to permit enquiry.

   Sif. Were they not missing both? both at one hour?
Say, for thou hast enquir'd ; is Paulet found?

   Beauf. sen. He is not : but my son perhaps, whom zeal
To clear a much-lov'd sister's injur'd fame

Eager impels to strictest inquisition,
May bring some tidings.

 Sif. May kind Heaven direct
His steps where lurks their covert shame from day,
And from my just revenge.

 Beauf. sen. Still, still thy rage
With weak, precarious inference concludes
Their unprov'd guilt. Be calm, and answer me.
Think'st thou thy wife, if bent on loose designs,
Would madly join an infant in her flight,
To impede her steps, and aggravate her shame?

 Sif. O my confusion! where, where is my child?
Alas, I had forgot the harmless innocent!
Bring to my arms the poor deserted babe!
He knows no crime, and guiltless of offence
Shall put his little hands into my breast,
And ease a father's bosom of its sorrows.

 Beauf. sen. Unhappy man! that comfort is deny'd
  thee.

 Sif. What means my father? Speak—yet ah, take
  heed!
My heart already is too deeply pierc'd,
To bear another wound—What of my child?

 Beauf. sen. That he's the partner of his mother's
  flight,
Should calm, not raise the tempest of thy grief—
For proves it not by consequence direct,
Some secret injury, not guilt, hath driven
My hapless daughter from her husband's roof?

 Sif. What injury, what crime could love like mine

Commit against her? Was she not more dear,
More precious to my heart, than the warm flood
Which feeds its vital motion?

　　Beauf. sen. Ev'n that love,
If open to the tales of calumny,
Might wound her virtue with unjust suspicion.
Besides, to rashness and credulity
Shadows are dæmons, and a weak surmise
Authentic proof. Who's her accuser?

　　Sif. One
Whose taintless honour, and unshaken truth,
Have oft been try'd, and ever stood approv'd.
He, Sir, whose friendship, with reluctant grief,
At length disclos'd my shame, was honest Glanville:
Report from vulgar breath I had despis'd.

　　Beauf. sen. So may high Heaven deal mercy to my
　　　　child,
As I believe him treacherous and base.

Enter BEAUFORT *Junior.*

　　Beauf. sen. Here comes my son—What means this
　　　　look of terror?

　　Beauf. jun. I fear, my father, some dread mischief—
　　　　Ha!—
Is he return'd!—Now may the powers avert
This dire suspicion that strikes thro' my heart!
Tell, I conjure thee tell me—where's my sister?
Thou hast not murder'd her!

　　Sif. Good Heaven! what means
My brother's dreadful words? Murder my wife!

Speak, quickly speak!—My heart shrinks up with
     horror!
Whence are thy apprehensions?

Beauf. sen. My dear son,
Keep not thy father on the rack of doubt,
But speak thy fears.

Beauf. jun. What fate may have befallen
My injur'd sister, Heaven and thou best know—
But Paulet, whom thy fierce revenge pursu'd,
This night is murder'd.

Sif. Ha! what say'st thou?—Paulet!
Is Paulet dead? How know'st thou he is murder'd?

Beauf. jun. In the dark path which to the cloister
     leads,
His sword is found, and bloody marks appear,
That speak the deed too plain.

Sif. But where's my wife?
Was not she with him? Went they not together?

Beauf. jun. Together! no. The villain Glanville's
     false!
My sister is traduc'd.

Sif. False! Glanville false!—
What!—Paulet murder'd!—and my wife traduc'd!
Rack me, ye furies! tear me joint from joint!
Your pangs are nothing—I have done a deed,
No tortures can atone! Tremendous Power!
What tempest wrapt in darkness now prepares
To burst on my devoted head? What crime
Unknown, or unrepented, points me out,
The mark distinguish'd of peculiar vengeance?

Why turns the gracious all-benignant eye
Averse from me? O guide my steps to find
Where lurks this hidden mischief—

   Beauf. jun. Lurks it not
In thine own breast?

   Beauf. sen. My son, forbear.

   Sif. Art thou,
My brother, so unkind! Would I have stabb'd
Thy heart, when breaking with convulsive pangs
Of dreadful doubt?—But I deserve unkindness—
I was unkind, was cruel to Cleone—
Yet lead me to her arms—tho' wrong'd, abus'd,
She like offended Heaven, will still forgive.
My friend too, my best friend is murder'd! Oh,
What hand accurst hath wrought this web of wo?
Support me, mercy! 'tis too much, too much!
But let distraction come, and from my brain
Tear out the seat of memory, that I
No more may think, no more may be a wretch!

   Beauf. sen. Be calm, my son. When Heaven's high
          hand afflicts,
Submission best becomes us—nor let man,
The child of weakness, murmur.

   Sif. O my father!
Thee too my rashness hath undone! Thou, thou
Wilt join with Heaven to curse me! but I kiss
The rod of chastisement, and in the dust
Resign'd, a prostrate suppliant, beg for mercy.

   Beauf. sen. Moderate the grief
Which thus unmans thee—Rouse thee to the search

Of these dark deeds—and Heaven direct our footsteps.
Hath not suspicion whisper'd to thy heart,
That he, this Glanville, whom thy friendship trusts
With confidence intire, may yet be false?

   Sif. Till this dread hour, suspicion of his truth
Ne'er touch'd my breast—Now doubt and horror raise
Distraction in my soul.

   Beauf. sen. All-gracious Power!
Look on our sorrows with a pitying eye!
My feeble heart sinks in me—But do thou
Bear up against this tide of wo: I trust,
If goodness dwell in heaven, my child is safe.
Perhaps she seeks the shelter of these arms,
And we have miss'd her in th' entangled wood.
With speed dispatch immediate messengers
Through different paths, with strictest search to trace
Cleone's steps, or find thy murder'd friend.
My son, I charge thee, see this well perform'd.

   Beauf. jun. I will not fail.   [*Exit* Beaufort *jun.*

   Beauf. sen. Mean while let us observe
Each motion, word, and look of this fell fiend;
So may we best detect him; and his schemes,
Tho' gloss'd with saint-like show (if much I err not),
Will soon in all their horrors stand reveal'd. [*Exeunt.*

SCENE III.

Changes to the Wood. Enter CLEONE *and her Child.*

   Cle. Whence do these terrors seize my sinking heart?

Since guilt I know not, wherefore know I fear?
And yet these silent shadowy scenes awake
Strange apprehensions. Guardian powers! protect
My weakness! Hark! what noise is that?—All still.
It was but fancy.—Yet methought the howl
Of distant wolves broke on the ear of night,
Doubling the desert's horror.

   Child. O I'm frighted!
Why do you speak and look so strangely at me?

   Cle. I will not fright my love. Come, let's go on—
We've but a little way—Save us, ye Powers!

     Enter RAGOZIN *with a Dagger and a Mask on.*

        [*Cleone flies with her Child, he follows.*
   Rag. Stop—for thou fly'st in vain.

   Cle. [*Within the scenes.*] Help! Mercy! Save!
Kill not my infant! Murder! O my child!

    [*She retreats back to the Scene, and falls in a swoon.*

     Re-enter RAGOZIN.

   Rag. She too is dead!—I fear'd that blow was
     short—
But hark! what noise?—I must not be detected—
No time to bury 'em now—be that his care.— [*Exit.*

   Cle. [*Waking from her trance.*] Where have I been?
     What horrid hand hath stamp'd
This dreadful vision on my brain? O Death!
Have I not gain'd thy mansions? Am I still
In this bad world? What ails my heart? my head?
Was not my child here with me? Sure he was—

And some foul dæmon terrifies my soul
With fears of murder.   Gracious Heaven, forbid!
Conduct my steps, kind Providence, to where
My little wanderer strays, that I may know
This horror in my mind is but a dream.   [*Exit.*

SCENE IV.

*Changes to an adjoining Part of the Wood, and discovers
the Child murder'd.   Enter* CLEONE.

Cle. O fearful silence! Not a sound returns,
Save the wild echoes of my own sad cries,
To my affrighted ear!—My child! my child!
Where art thou wander'd—where beyond the reach
Of thy poor mother's voice!—Yet while above
The God of justice dwells, I will not deem
The bloody vision true.   Heaven hath not left me—
There truth is known, well known—and see my love!
See, where upon the bank its weary'd limbs
Lie stretch'd in sleep.   In sleep! O agony!
Blast not my senses with a sight like this!
'Tis blood! 'tis death! my child, my child is murder'd!

   [*Falls down by her child, kissing it and weeping. Then
     raising herself on her arm, after a dead silence,
     and looking by degrees more and more wild, she pro-
     ceeds in a distracted manner.*

Hark! hark! lie still, my love!—For all the world
Don't stir!—'Tis Glanville, and he'll murder us!
Stay, stay—I'll cover thee with boughs—don't fear—

I'll call the little lambs, and they shall bring
Their softest fleece to shelter thee from cold.
There, there—lie close—he shall not see—no, no;
I'll tell him 'tis an angel I have hid.   [*She rises up.*
Where is he? soft!—he's gone, he's gone, my love,
And shall not murder thee.—Poor innocent!
'Tis fast asleep. Well thought! I'll steal away,
Now while he slumbers—pick wild berries for him,
And bring a little water in my hand—
Then, when he wakes, we'll seat us on the bank,
And sing all night.

ACT IV. SCENE I.

A Room in SIFROY's *House.* GLANVILLE, *and*
ISABELLA.

Glanville.

BETRAY'D! by whom betray'd? By thy vain fear.
How curs'd is he who treads on danger's path,
Entangled with a woman! Fool! alone
I had been safe.

  Isab. Yet hear me—On my life,
No word from me hath 'scap'd. We may perchance
Be yet secure.

  Glan. Perchance! And do our lives
Depend on fickle chance? But speak—proceed—
Whence are thy fears?

  Isab. In close concealment hid,
This moment I o'erheard a whisper'd scheme
Of seizing thee.

F

Glan. Confusion! Can it be?
Can Ragozin, the villain, have betray'd me?

Isab. I fear he hath. Where is he?

Glan. Not return'd
From Baden wood, to ascertain the deed
That crowns our business. Were but that secure,
My tortur'd soul, torn on the rack of doubt,
Might yet feel peace. How wears the time?

Isab. Two hours
Are wanting yet to midnight.

Glan. Where's Sifroy?

Isab. With Beaufort. But perplexing doubts distract
His reason, that all power to act forsakes him.
Still farther to alarm—deep-stain'd with gore,
The sword of Paulet's found, and other marks
That speak him murder'd.

Glan. That's beyond my wish:
And tells but what I wanted to proclaim.

Isab. Proclaim! What mean'st thou? Doth it not
     conduce
To our detection? Doth it not confirm
Their dark suspicions?

Glan. The short line, alas,
Of thy weak thought, in vain would sound the depth
Of my designs. But rest thee well assur'd
I have foreseen, and am prepar'd to meet
All possible events.

Isab. O grant, good Heaven—
Great God! how dreadful 'tis to be engag'd
In what we dare not pray that Heaven may prosper!

Glan. Curse on thy boding tongue! Let me not hear
Its superstitious weakness—Hush! who comes?
No more—'tis Ragozin—Now sleep distrust.
First let me learn if he hath done the deed,
If not, I am betray'd, and will awake
In vengeance on his falsehood.

Enter RAGOZIN.

Glan. Speak, my friend—
Cleone and her child—say quickly—how disposed?

Rag. To heav'n remov'd, no longer they obstruct
Our views on earth.

Glan. Speak plainly—are they dead?

Rag. Both dead.

Glan. Swear, swear to this! And by all hope
Of that reward which urg'd thee to the deed,
Swear thou hast not betray'd me!

Rag. Whence arise
These base suspicions? I disdain that crime!
Tho' branded with the name of an assassin,
I am not yet so mean as to betray.

Glan. Distraction!—may I trust thee?

Rag. As thou wilt.

Glan. [*Pausing.*] It must be so—we still are safe:
and this
Pretence of strong suspicion is no more
Than subtil artifice, contriv'd to draw
Th' unwary to confession.

Rag. 'Tis no more.

Glan. Nor will I more than with a just contempt

Regard it. All our deeds of blood are done.
What now remains, the law shall execute.

   Rag. What's thy intent?

   Glan. The thrust thus aim'd at me,
Shall deeply pierce Sifroy's unguarded bosom.
Thy aid once more, as witness to his threats.

   Rag. Freely I would, but safety now requires
That I abscond. The stipulated sum,
Forgive me therefore, if I claim this night.

   Glan. 'Tis thine. But hark!—retire—I hear his
      step—
One moment wait—at his return, 'tis thine.

   Rag. [*Aside.*] Curs'd chance! Were I possess'd of
      my reward,
Who would might wait thee now—nor will I more
Than some short moments rest unsatisfied.   [*Exit.*

Enter SIFROY.

   Sif. [*Not seeing* Glanville.] O happiness! thou frail,
      thou fading flower,
Whose culture mocks all human toil, farewell!
But I, blind madman! by the roots have pluck'd
Thy sweetness from my bosom. My dear love!
Where wanders now thy wrong'd, thy helpless virtue?
On what cold stone reclines thy drooping head,
While trickling tears call thy Sifroy inhuman?
Deluded wretch! why did my greedy ear
Catch the rank poison of suspicion's breath,
And to my tortur'd brain convey distraction?

Glan. [*Advancing to him.*]　Are thus my faithful
　　　services repaid ?

Are the plain truths my undisguising heart
In friendship told, already deem'd no more
Than vile suggestions of designing falsehood ?

Sif. Villain, they are !—Thou know'st them false
　　　as hell !

Where is my wife ?—O traitor ! thou hast plung'd
My soul into perdition !

Glan. Rather say,
That he who led astray the willing wife,
Thy folly doats on—he—

Sif. Blasphemer ! stop
Thy impious tongue ! The breast of that dear saint
Enshrines a soul as spotless as her form.
Said'st thou not, slanderer ! that my love was fled
With Paulet ?

Glan. True : I did.

Sif. Art thou not sure
That this is false ? Hast thou no dreadful cause
To know it cannot be ?

Glan. None. Thou, perhaps,
Whose bloody errand I indeed have heard
Already is accomplish'd—thou, 'tis true,
May'st know that they are parted : 'twas the deed
Thou flew'st thus swiftly to perform. But how
Doth that impeach the truth of her elopement ?
That thou hast murder'd him, acquits not her.

Sif. That　I　have　murder'd !—I !—Pernicious
　　　wretch !

What dark design, by blackest fiends inspir'd,
Lurks in thy treacherous soul ? Tremendous Power !
Have I then sinn'd beyond all hope of mercy ?
Must the deep phial of thy vengeance, pour'd
On my devoted head, be pour'd from him ?
But all thy ways are just ! To him I gave
That credit which I ow'd my injur'd love—
He now, by thy supreme decree, stands forth
The avenger of my crime.

Enter BEAUFORT *senior, Officers, &c.*

Beauf. sen. Seize there your victim.

Glan. What means this outrage ?—Upon what pre-
        tence—

Beauf. sen. The bloody hand of murder points out
        thee

To strong suspicion. Turn'st thou pale ?—O wretch !
Thy guilt drinks up thy blood.

Glan. Not guilt, but rage !
Who dares accuse me ?

Beauf. sen. I. Where's Paulet ? where
My daughter ? who thou basely said'st were fled
Together ?

Glan. That his poinard found the way
To part their steps, impeaches not my truth.

Beauf. sen. His poinard !

Glan. His. I should have scorn'd to charge
The man, whose honour I think deeply wrong'd ;
But my own life attempted thus, demands
That truth should rise to light. Cam'st thou not here,

Driven by the fury of a dire revenge?
What other motive urg'd thy desperate haste?

Sif. Insidious slave! hast thou insnar'd my soul
By treacherous arts?—Hast thou with falsehood vile
Inflam'd this hapless breast?—And would'st thou now
Infer my guilt, from my provok'd resentment?

Glan. Lean'd I on feeble inference—I would ask,
What cause have I to seek this Paulet's blood?
'Twas not my wife, my daughter, he seduc'd!
How has he injur'd me? But I reject
These trivial pleas—I build on certain proof.

Beauf. sen. What proof?

Glan. The strongest—his own hand and seal
Fixt to the firm resolve, that he alone
                              [*Shewing the letter.*
Would do the righteous deed—for so his rage
Calls Paulet's murder.

Beauf. sen. Ha! What can I think!
Unhappy man! and hast thou to the crime
Of rash suspicion, added that of murder?

Sif. My father, hear thy son; I plead not for
My life, but justice.—That I am a wretch,
Groaning beneath the weight of Heaven's just ire—
That snared and caught in meditated wiles,
I banish'd from my house a guiltless wife—
That burning with revenge, I flew to quench
My wrath in Paulet's blood—all this I own.
But by the sacred eye of Providence!
That views each human step, and still detects

The murderer's deed; of this imputed crime
My heart is ignorant, my hands are clear.

 Beauf. sen. I wish thee innocent—

 Glan. Have then my words
No weight ? and is his own attesting hand
No proof against him ? Is her secret flight
An accident ? No more—O partial man !
To hide thy daughter's shame, thou seek'st my life.
But I appeal from thee to public justice.

 Beauf. sen. To that thou art consign'd : and may the
    hand
Of strict enquiry drag to open day
All secret guilt, tho' shame indelible
Should brand a daughter nearest to my heart.
Heaven aid my search! I seek not blood, but truth.
Guard safe your prisoner to the magistrate,
I'll follow you. The justice thou demand'st,
Thou shalt not want.

 Glan. 'Tis well : I ask no more.
Let Ragozin, let Isabella too
Attend the magistrate—on them I call
To clear my slander'd name.

 Beauf. sen. It shall be so.
Take them this instant to your strictest care.
Thou too, Sifroy, be ready to attend.

 Sif. O think not I will leave him, till full proof
Condemn him or acquit.

 Beauf. sen. The cause demands it.
     [*Exeunt Officers with* Glanville *guarded.*

Sif. Whence has the miscreant this unusual firmness?
Can guilt be free from terror?

Beauf. sen. No, my son:
And thro' the mask of smooth hypocrisy,
Methinks I see conceal'd a trembling heart.
If he be true, my daughter must be false:
If he be guiltless, who hath murder'd Paulet?

Sif. There, there, thank Heaven! my hands are
      innocent.
But oh, my love!—Conduct me where she strays
Forlorn and comfortless! Alas, who knows—
Her tender heart perhaps this moment breaks
With my unkindness! Wretch! what hast thou lost!

Enter BEAUFORT *junior.*

Beauf. jun. Thy soul's sweet peace!—Never, no
      never more
To be regain'd!—Shame, anguish, and despair
Shall haunt thy future hours! Severe remorse
Shall strike his vulture talons thro' thy heart,
And rend thy vital threads.

Beauf. sen. What means my son?

Sif. My brother!—If I may conjure thee yet
By that dear name.—

Beauf. jun. Thou may'st not—I disclaim it.

Sif. Why dost thou still alarm my shuddering soul
With rising terrors?

Beauf. sen. My dear son, relieve
Thy father from this dread suspence!

Beauf. jun. O Sir! how shall I speak! or in what
      words

Unfold the horrors of this night?—My sister—
Lost to her wretched self—thro' dreary wilds
Wanders distracted—void of reason's light
To guide her devious feet.

    Beauf. sen. Support me, Heaven!
Then every hope is fled!—Thy will be done!—
Where is my child? Where was she found?

    Beauf. jun. Alas!
Of soul too delicate, too soft to bear
Unjust reproach, and undeserved shame,
Distraction seiz'd her in the gloom of night,
As passing thro' the wood she sought the arms
Of a protecting father.

    Sif. Do I live?
Is such a wretch permitted still to breathe?
Why opens not this earth? Why sleeps above
The lightning's vengeful blast? Is Heaven unjust?
Or am I still reserv'd for deeper wo?
I hope not mercy—that were impious—
Pour then on my bare head, ye ministers
Of wrath! your hottest vengeance—

    Beauf. jun. Stop—forbear—
Nor imprecate that vengeance, which unseen
Already hangs o'er thy devoted life.
Thou know'st not yet the measure of thy wo.
Thy child, thy lovely babe, a bloody corse,
Lies breathless by his frantic mother's side—
Much to be fear'd, by her own hand destroy'd,
When reason in her brain had lost dominion.

    Sif. My child too gone!—Then misery is complete—
O my torn heart!—Is there in heaven no pity?

None, none for me! The wrongs of all I lov'd
To heaven ascending, bar th' eternal gates,
And close the ear of mercy 'gainst my prayer.
But fate's last bolt is thrown, and I am curst
Beyond all power to sharpen torture's pang.
Yes, I am scorn'd, abandon'd, and cast out
By heaven and earth!—I must not call thee father—
I have undone thee, robb'd thee of the name:
And now, myself am childless, and undone.

    Beauf. sen. Forbear, my son, to aggravate thy grief,
Already too severe. Kind Providence
May yet restore, and harmonize her mind.

    Sif. May Heaven pour blessings on thy reverend head
For that sweet hope! but say, where shall I see her?—
How bear the dreadful sight!

    Beauf. jun. Dreadful indeed!
On the cold earth they found her laid: her head,
Supported on her arm, hung o'er her child,
The image of pale grief, lamenting innocence.
Sometimes she speaks fond words, and seems to smile
On the dead babe as 'twere alive.—Now, like
The melancholy bird of night, she pours
A soft and melting strain, as if to soothe
Its slumbers: and now clasps it to her breast,
Cries Glanville is not here—fear not, my love,
He shall not come—Then wildly throws her eyes
Around, and in the tenderest accent calls
Aloud on thee, to save her from dishonour!

    Sif. Haste, let us haste—distracted thus, she grows

Still dearer, still more precious to my soul!
O let me soothe her sorrows into peace.

 Beauf. sen. Stay—calls she frequently on Glanville's
   name?

 Beauf. jun. So they report who found her.

 Beauf. sen. Left they her
Alone?

 Beauf. jun. No: but all arts to court her thence
   were vain.

 Beauf. sen. Thither with speed this moment let us fly.
Let Glanville too attend.　From the wild words
Of madness and delirium, he who struck
From darkness light—may call discovery forth,
To guide our footsteps.

 Beauf. jun. Just is your resolve,
And I will follow you—but have receiv'd
Intelligence of Paulet that imports us.

 Sif. Of Paulet! of my friend! What may it be?

 Beauf. jun. As yet I'm ignorant.

 Beauf. sen. To gain us light,
Be no means left untry'd.　　　　　[*Exit* Beauf. jun.

 Sif. But haste, we linger.
Yet whither can I fly? where seek for peace?
In its most tender vein my heart is wounded!
Had I been smote in any other part,
I could have borne with firmness; but in thee,
My wrong'd, my ruin'd love, I bleed to death.

       [*Exeunt.*

ACT V. SCENE I.

The Wood. CLEONE *is discovered sitting by her dead child; over whom she hath form'd a little bower of shrubs and branches of trees. She seems very busy in picking little sprigs from a bough in her hand.*

Cleone sings.

> *SWEETER than the damask rose*
> *Was his lovely breast;*
> *There, O let me there repose,*
> *Sigh, sigh, and sink to rest.*

Did I not love him? who can say I did not?
My heart was in his bosom, but he tore
It out, and cast it from him—Yet I lov'd—
And he more lovely seem'd to that fond heart,
Than the bright cherub sailing on the skirts
Of yonder cloud, th' inhabitant of heaven.

Enter SIFROY, BEAUFORT *Senior,* ISABELLA, GLANVILLE, RAGOZIN, *Officers, &c.*

　Beauf. sen. This is the place—And see my hapless
　　child!
Why, gracious Heaven! why have I liv'd to feel
This dreadful moment? Soft I pray ye tread—
And let us well observe her speech and action.
　Sif. Have I done this!—and do I live!—My heart

G

Drops blood! but to thy guidance I will bend,
And in forc'd silence smother killing grief.

　　Glan. [*Aside.*] Did'st thou not tell me, villain, she
　　　　was dead?

　　Rag. [*Aside.*] I was deceiv'd—by Heav'n, I thought
　　　　her so.

　　Glan. [*Aside.*] May hell reward thee.

　　Beauf. sen. Stay—she rises—hush!

　　Cle. Soft! soft! he stirs——

O, I have wak'd him—I have wak'd my child!
And when false Glanville knows it, he again
Will murder him.

　　Beauf. sen. Mark that!

　　Glan. And are the words
Of incoherent madness to convict me?

　　Sif. They are the voice of Heaven, detecting murder!
Yes, villain! thy infernal aim appears.

　　Cle. No, no; all still—As undisturb'd he sleeps
As the stolen infant rock'd in th' eagle's nest.
I'll call the red-breast, and the nightingale,
Their pious bills once cover'd little babes,
And sung their dying dirge. Again, sweet birds!
Again pour forth your melancholy notes,
And soothe once more that innocence ye love.

　　Sif. On that enchanting voice, how my fond heart
Hath hung with rapture!—now too deeply pierc'd
I die upon the sound. 　　　　[*He advances towards her.*
My dearest love,
Behold thy own Sifroy, return'd to calm
Thy griefs! and pour into thy wounded mind
The healing balm of tenderness!

Cle. [*Frighted and trembling.*] Sweet Heaven,
Protect me! O, if you have pity, save
My infant!—Cast away that bloody steel!
And on my knees I'll kiss the gentle hand
That spar'd my child!—Glanville shall never know
But we are dead—In this lone wood we'll live,
And I no more will seek my husband's house.
And yet I never wrong'd him! never indeed!

    Sif. I know thou didst not—Look upon me, love!
Dost thou not know me? I am thy Sifroy—
Thy husband—Do not break my heart—O speak!
That look will kill me!

    Beauf. sen. My dear child! Look up—
Look on thy father! Am I too forgotten?
Is every filial trace in thy poor brain
Defac'd—She knows us not!—May Heaven, my son,
Lend thee its best support! For me—my days
Are few; nor can my sorrows date be long
Protracted.

    Sif. Say not so! Must I become
The murderer of all I hold most dear?

    Cle. Yes—yes—a husband once—a father too
I had—but lost, quite lost—deep in my brain
Bury'd they lie——In heaps of rolling sand—
I cannot find them.

    Sif. O heart-rending grief!
How is that fair, that amiable mind,
Disjointed, blasted by the fatal rage
Of one rash moment! [*She goes to her child, he follows.*
Let sweet pity veil

The horrors of this scene from every eye !
My child ! my child ! hide, hide me from that sight!
　　　　　　　　　　　　　　　[Turns away.

　　Cle. Stay, stay——for you are good, and will not
　　　　hurt
My lamb.   Alas, you weep—why should you weep ?
I am his mother, yet I cannot weep.
Have you more pity than a mother feels ?
But I shall weep no more——my heart is cold.

　　Sif. [*Falling on his knees.*] O mitigate thy wrath,
　　　　good Heaven ! Thou know'st
My weakness—lay not on thy creature more
Than he can bear : Restore her, O restore !
But if it must not be—if I am doom'd
To stand a dreadful warning to deter
Frail man from sudden rage—Almighty Power,
Then take, in mercy take, this wretched life !

　　　　[*As he rises,* Isabella *comes forward and throws her-
　　　　self at his feet.*

　　Isab. Hear, hear me, Sir ; my very heart is pierc'd !
And my shock'd soul, beneath a load of guilt,
Sinks down in terrors unsupportable.
'Tis Heaven impels me to reveal the crimes,
In which a fatal passion has involv'd me.
Protect me, save me from his desperate rage !

　　　　[Glanville *suddenly pulls out a short dagger which he
　　　　had conceal'd in his bosom ; and attempts to stab her :
　　　　one of the Officers wrenches it from him.*

　　Beauf. sen. Ha ! seize the dagger !

　　Sif. Hold thy murderous hand !

Rag. [*Aside.*] All is betray'd—for me no safety now,
But sudden flight.   [*He endeavours to withdraw.*

Sif. Stop—seize—detain that slave!
Th' attempt to fly bespeaks him an accomplice.
          [*He is seized by the Officers.*

Isab. [*To* Glanville.] Tremble, O wretch!—Thou
          seest that Heaven is just,
Nor suffers even ourselves to hide our deeds.
To death I yield—nor hope, nor wish for life—
Permit me to reveal some dreadful truths,
And I shall die content. Thy hapless wife,
Chaste as the purest angel of the sky,
By Glanville is traduc'd—by him betray'd.
Paulet is murder'd—and by his device,
The lovely child. Seduc'd by his vile arts,
And by the flattering hopes of wealth ensnar'd,
Distraɕting thought! I have destroy'd my soul.

Beauf. sen. Why, why so far from virtue didst thou
          stray,
That to compassionate thy wretched fate,
Almost is criminal?
[*To* Glanville.] But canst thou bear—
Can thy hard heart support this dreadful scene?

Glan. I know the worst, and am prepar'd to meet it.
That wretch hath seal'd my death. And had I but
Aveng'd her timorous perfidy—the rest
I'd leave to fate; and neither should lament
My own, nor pity yours.

Sif. Inhuman savage!
But justice shall exert her keenest scourge,

And wake to terror thy unfeeling heart.
Guard them to safe confinement.—Killing sight!
Behold that piteous object!—Her dumb grief
Speaks to my heart unutterable wo!
Horror is in her silence—[*He goes to her*] My dear love!
Look, look upon me! Let these tears prevail,
And with thy reason, wake thy pity too.

Cle. Again you weep—But had you lost a wife,
As I a husband, you might weep indeed!
Or had you lost so sweet a boy as mine,
'Twould break your heart!

Sif. Her words are pointed steel!
Have I not lost a wife?—lost a sweet boy?
Indeed I have!- Myself too murder'd them!

   Cle. That was unkind—Why did you so?—But
        hush!
Let no one talk of murder—I was kill'd—
My husband murder'd me—but I forgave him.

Sif. I cannot, cannot bear!—O torture! torture!

Beauf. sen. Collect thyself, and with the humble eye
Of patient hope, look up to Heaven resign'd.

Sif. Hope! where is hope!—Alas, no hope for me!
On downy pinions, lo! to heaven she flies—
To realms of bliss—where I must never come!
Terrors are mine—and from the depths below,
Despair looks out and beckons me to sink!

Beauf. sen. Assuage thy grief! call reason to thy aid,
Perhaps we yet may save her precious life;
At least delay not, by some gentle means,
To soothe her to return.

Sif. May soft persuasion dwell upon thy lips!
But ah, can tears or arguments avail,
When reason marks not?

Enter BEAUFORT *junior.*

Beauf. jun. Where, where is my sister?

Beauf. sen. Alas! the melancholy sight will pierce
Thy inmost soul!—But do not yet disturb her.
Distraction o'er her memory hangs a cloud,
That hides us from her.

Sif. My dearest brother! can thy heart receive
The wretch, who robb'd it of a sister's love?

Beauf. jun. I do forgive thee all——Alas, my bro-
        ther!

Most basely wert thou wrong'd. But truth is found—
Paulet, tho' wounded, yet escap'd with life.

Sif. Then Heaven is just--But tell me, how escap'd--

Beauf. jun. Thou shalt know all—But stay! my
        sister speaks—

Cle. [*Coming forward.*] O who hath done it!—who
        hath done this deed

Of death?—My child is murder'd—my sweet babe
Bereft of life!—Thou Glanville! thou art he!
Remorseless fiend! destroy a child! an infant!——
Monster, forbear!——See, see the little heart
Bleeds on his dagger's point!

[*Looking down to the earth.*

But lo! the furies!—the black fiends of hell
Have seiz'd the murderer! look; they tear his heart—
That heart which had no pity! Hark; he shrieks——

3

His eye-balls glare—his teeth together gnash
In bitterness of anguish—while the fiends
Scream in his frighted ear—*Thou shalt not murder!*

 Beauf. sen. What dreadful visions terrify her brain!
To interrupt her must relieve.—Speak to her.

 Sif. My dearest love!—cast but one look upon us!

 Cle. [*Looking up to heaven.*] Is that my infant?—
   Whither do ye bear
My bleeding babe? Not yet. O mount not yet,
Ye sons of light, but take me on your wings,
With my sweet innocent—I come! I come!
    [*Her father and brother take hold of her.*
Yet hold; where is my husband—my Sifroy?
Will not he follow? Will he quite forsake
His poor lost wife?—O tell him I was true! [*Swoons.*

 Beauf. sen. Alas, she faints!—I fear the hand of
   death
Is falling on her. Gently bear her up.

 Sif. O God! my heart—
My heart-strings break!—Did not her dying words
Dwell on my name? Did not her latest sigh
Breathe tenderness for me?—for me, the wretch,
Whose rash suspicion, whose intemperate rage,
Abandon'd her to shame!—Hah! gracious Heaven!
Does she not move? Does not returning light
Dawn in her feeble eye? Her opening lips
Breathe the sweet hope of life!

 Cle. Where have I been?
What dreadful dreams have floated in my brain!

 Beauf. sen. How fares my child?

Cle. O faint! exceeding faint!
My father!—my dear father!—Do I wake?
And am I, am I in a father's arms?
My brother too—O happy!

Beauf. jun. My dear sister!

Sif. Transporting rapture! Will my love return
To life? to reason too? indulgent Power!

Cle. What sound, what well-known voice is that I
          hear!
Support me, raise me to his long-lost arms!
It is my husband! my Sifroy! my love!
Alas, too faint—I never more shall rise.

Sif. Ah! do not wound me, do not pierce my heart
With any thought so dreadful! Art thou given
In mockery only to my longing arms?
Raise up thy head, my love! lean on my breast,
And whisper to my soul thou wilt not die.

Cle. How thy sweet accents soothe the pangs of death
Witness ye angels! thus in thy dear arms
To die, my faithful love, and spotless truth
Confirm'd, was all my wish! Where is my father?
Let me but take his blessings up to heaven,
And I shall go with confidence!

Beauf. sen. My child—
My darling child!—May that pure bliss, just heaven
Bestows upon departed saints, be thine!

Cle. Farewell, my brother! comfort and support
Our father's feeble age—To heal his grief
Will give thy sister's dying moments ease.

Sif. Talk not of death!—We must not, must not
      part!

Good Heaven! her dying agonies approach!

   Cle. The keenest pang of death, is that I feel
For thy surviving wo.—Adieu, my love!
I do entreat thee with my last, last breath,
Restrain thy tears—nor let me grieve to think
Thou feel'st a pain I cannot live to cure.

   Sif. Might'st thou but live, how light were every
      pain
Fate could inflict!

   Cle. It will not be!—I faint—

My spirits fail—farewell—receive me, Heaven. [*Dies.*

   Sif. She's gone!—for ever gone!—Those lovely
      eyes
Are clos'd in death—no more to look on me!
My fate is fix'd, and in this tortur'd breast
Anguish—remorse—despair—must ever dwell.

   Beauf. sen. Offended power! at length with pitying
      eyes
Look on our misery! Cut short this thread,
That links my soul too long to wretched life!

   And let mankind, taught by his hapless fate,
   Learn one great truth, experience finds too late;
   That dreadful ills from rash resentment flow,
   And sudden passions end in lasting wo.

                  [*Exeunt.*

THE END.

EPILOGUE,
By WILLIAM SHENSTONE, Esq.

Spoken by Mrs. BELLAMY.

WELL, Ladies—so much for the Tragic stile—
And now, the custom is—to make you smile.
" *To make us smile, I hear* Flippanta *say,*
" *Yes—we have* smil'd *indeed—thro' half the play :*
" *We* always *laugh when Bards, demure and sly,*
" *Bestow such mighty pains—to make us* cry.
" *And truly, to bring sorrow to a crisis,*
" *Mad-folks, and murder'd babes are*—shrewd *devices.*

" *The Captain gone three years—and* then *to blame*
" *The vestal conduct of his virtuous dame !—*
" *What* French, *what* English *bride would think it treason,*
" *When thus accus'd—to give the brute some reason ?*
" *Out of my house—this night, forsooth—depart !*
" *A* modern *wife had said—With all my heart :*
" *But think not, haughty Sir, I'll go alone !*
" *Order your coach—conduct me safe to town—*
" *Give me my jewels—wardrobe—and my maid—*
" *And pray take care my pin-money be paid :*
" *Else know, I wield a pen—and, for his glory,*
" *My dear's domestic feats may shine in story !*

" *Then for the Child—the tale was truly sad—*
" *But who for such a bantling would run mad ?*
" *What wife, at midnight hour inclin'd to roam,*
" *Would fondly drag her little chit from* home ?
" *What has a mother with her child to do ?*
" *Dear brats—the* Nursery's *the place for you !*"

Such are the strains of many a modish Fair !
Yet memoires—not of modern *growth—declare*
The time has been, *when modesty and truth*
Were deem'd additions to the charms of youth ;
Ere, in the dice-box, ladies found delight ;
Or swoon'd, for lack of cards, on Sunday-night ;
When women hid their necks, and veil'd their faces,
Nor romp'd, nor rak'd, nor star'd, at public places:
Nor took the airs of Amazons—for graces !
When plain domestic virtues were the mode ;
And wives ne'er dreamt of happiness abroad,
But cheer'd their offspring, shunn'd fantastic airs ;
And, with the joys *of wedlock, mixt the* cares.

Such modes are past—yet sure they merit praise ;
For marriage triumph'd *in those wassel days:*
No virgin sigh'd in vain ; no fears arose,
Lest holy wars should cause a dearth of beaux :
By chaste decorum, each, affection gain'd ;
By faith and fondness, what she won, maintain'd.

'*Tis yours, ye fair! to mend a thoughtless age,*
That scorns the press, the pulpit, and the stage!
To yield frail husbands no pretence *to stray:*
(Men will be rakes, if women lead the way).
To soothe—But truce with these preceptive lays;
The Muse, who, dazzled with your ancient praise,
On present worth, and modern beauty tramples,
Must own, she ne'er could boast more bright examples*.

* Addressing the Boxes.

H

Act I.   THE MINOR.

De Wilde pinx.ᵗ   Leney sculp.

Mr. ANGELO as Mrs. COLE.

*All shall have their call, as Mr. Squintum says,
sooner or later.*

London Printed for J.Bell British Library, Strand, Sept.ʳ 29.1792.

BRITISH
THEATRE

MINOR.

Mᵣˢ COLE.— MERCY ON US, WHERE DO
YOU EXPECT TO GO WHEN YOU DIE?

Act I.

Smirke pinxᵗ.   Leney sculp

London, Printed for J. Bell, British Library. Strand. Septʳ 29 1792.

THE MINOR.

A

COMEDY,

By SAMUEL FOOTE, Esq.

ADAPTED FOR

THEATRICAL REPRESENTATION,

AS PERFORMED AT THE

THEATRES-ROYAL,

DRURY-LANE AND COVENT-GARDEN.

REGULATED FROM THE PROMPT-BOOKS,
By Permission of the Managers.

" The Lines distinguished by inverted Commas, are omitted in the Representation."

LONDON :

Printed for the Proprietors, under the Direction of
JOHN BELL, British-Library, STRAND,
Bookseller to His Royal Highness the PRINCE of WALES.

MDCCXCII.

WILLIAM
DUKE OF DEVONSHIRE.
Lord Chamberlain of His Majesty's Household.

MY LORD,

THE MINOR, who is indebted for his appear-
ance on the Stage to your Grace's indulgence, begs
leave to desire your further protection, at his entering
into the world.

Though the allegiance due from the whole dra-
matic people to your Grace's station, might place this
address in the light of a natural tribute; yet, my
Lord, I should not have taken that liberty with the
Duke of Devonshire, if I could not at the same time,
plead some little utility in the design of my piece ;
and add, that the public approbation has stamped a
value on the execution.

The law, which threw the Stage under the absolute
government of a Lord Chamberlain, could not fail to
fill the minds of all the objects of that power with
very gloomy apprehensions ; they found themselves
(through their own licentiousness, it must be con
fessed) in a more precarious dependent state, than
any other of His Majesty's subjects. But when their
direction was lodged in the hands of a nobleman,
whose ancestors had so successfully struggled for
national liberty, they ceased to fear for their own.

It was not from a patron of the liberal arts they were to expect an oppressor; it was not from the friend of freedom, and of man, they were to dread partial monopolies, or the establishment of petty tyrannies.

Their warmest wishes are accomplished; none of their rights have been invaded, except what, without the first poetic authority, I should not venture to call a right, the Jus Nocendi.

Your tenderness, my Lord, for all the followers of the Muses, has been in no instance more conspicuous, than in your late favour to me, the meanest of their train; your Grace has thrown open (for those who are denied admittance into the Palaces of Parnassus) a cottage on its borders, where the unhappy migrants may be, if not magnificently, at least, hospitably entertained.

I shall detain your Grace no longer, than just to echo the public voice, that, for the honour, progress, and perfection of letters, your Grace may long continue their candid CENSOR, *who have always been their generous protector.*

I have the honour, my Lord, to be, with the greatest respect, and gratitude,

   Your Grace's most dutiful,

    Most obliged,

     And obedient Servant,

Ellestre,   *SAMUEL FOOTE.*

July 8, 1760.

THE MINOR.

THE Dramas of this Writer, having been founded upon the floating incidents and the characters of his own time, have no other claims upon posterity than what their keenness of wit and fertility of humour may give. Few of them are like Shakspere's Representations of General Nature. The Characters are not those of the Class, but the Individual, and when the original is snatched from our recollection, the copy is thereby abated of its principal power to please. They therefore depend more upon mimicry than just conception, and his personages will continue to be traditionally played in the manner that Foote, their creator, performed them.

This bar to his perpetuity of Fame affects the present Play less than most of his Collection. The Minor can be scarcely out of vogue while we have a BAWD in the Stews, an AUCTIONEER in the Rostrum, or a METHODIST in the Pulpit.

It may be desirable to transmit, that the Characters sketched under the appellations of *Mother Cole, Smirk,* and *Shift,* were very just imitations of the well-known Mother DOUGLAS, Mr. LANGFORD the Auctioneer, and GEORGE WHITFIELD, the Enthusiast.

The present Play was happily conducive to opening the eyes of Men upon the pernicious principles of the wretched Devotees of the Tabernacle. It is at all times dangerous to attack any mode of piety, but true devotion suffered little, it is believed, on the present occasion.

DRURY-LANE.

PERSONS IN THE INTRODUCTION.

Men.

FOOTE, - - - - - - ————
CANKER, - - - - - ————
SMART, - - - - - ————
PEARSE, - - - - - ————

IN THE COMEDY.

Men.

Sir WILLIAM WEALTHY, - -	Mr. Baddeley.
Mr. RICHARD WEALTHY, - -	Mr. Packer.
Sir GEORGE WEALTHY, -	Mr. Whitfield.
SHIFT, - - - - - -	Mr. Bannister, jun.
LOADER, - - - - -	Mr. R. Palmer.
DICK, - - - - - -	Mr. Burton.
TRANSFER, - - - -	————
SMIRK, - - - - -, -	Mr. Bannister, jun.

Women.

Mrs. COLE, - - - -	Mr. Bannister.
LUCY, - - - - -	Miss Collins.

COVENT-GARDEN.

Men.

Sir WILLIAM WEALTHY, -	Mr. Wewitzer.
Mr. RICHARD WEALTHY, -	Mr. Usher.
Sir GEORGE WEALTHY, -	Mr. Iliff.
SHIFT, - - -	Mr. Bannister, jun.
LOADER, - - -	Mr. R. Palmer.
DICK, - - -	Mr. Burton.
TRANSFER, - - - -	————
SMIRK, - - -	Mr. Bannister, jun.

Women.

Mrs. COLE, - - - -	Mr. Bannister.
LUCY, - - - -	Miss Heard.

THE MINOR.

INTRODUCTION.

Enter CANKER *and* SMART.

Smart.

BUT are you sure he has leave?

Cank. Certain.

Smart. I'm damn'd glad on't. For now we shall have a laugh either with him, or at him, it does not signify which.

Cank. Not a farthing.

Smart. D'you know his scheme?

Cank. Not I.——But is not the door of the Little Theatre open?

Smart. Yes.——Who is that fellow that seems to stand centry there?

Cank. By his tattered garb, and meagre visage, he must be one of the troop.

Smart. I'll call him.——Halloo, Mr.——

Enter PEARSE.

What, is there any thing going on over the way?

Pearse. A rehearsal.

Smart. Of what?

Pearse. A new piece.

Smart. Foote's?

Pearse. Yes.

Cank. Is he there?

Pearse. He is.

Smart. Zounds, let us go and see what he is about.

Cank. With all my heart.

Smart. Come along then.   [*Exeunt.*

Enter FOOTE, *and an Actor.*

Foote. Sir, this will never do; you must get rid of your high notes, and country cant.   Oh, 'tis the true strolling.———

Enter SMART *and* CANKER.

Smart. Ha, ha, ha! what, hard at it, my boy!——— Here's your old friend Canker and I come for a peep. Well, and hey, what is your plan?

Foote. Plan!

Smart. Ay, what are your characters? Give us your groupe; how is your cloth fill'd?

Foote. Characters!

Smart. Ay.—— Come, come, communicate. What, man, we will lend thee a lift. I have a damned fine original for thee, an aunt of my own, just come from

the North, with the true Newcastle bur in her throat ;
and a nose and a chin.——I am afraid she is not well
enough known : but I have a remedy for that. I'll
bring her the first night of your piece, place her in
a conspicuous station, and whisper the secret to the
whole house. That will be damned fine, won't it ?

Foote. Oh, delicious !

Smart. But don't name me.—For if she smokes me
for the author, I shall be dashed out of her codicil in
a hurry.

Foote. Oh, never fear me. But I should think your
uncle Tom a better character.

Smart. What, the politician ?

Foote. Aye ; that every day, after dinner, as soon
as the cloth is removed, fights the battle of Minden,
batters the French with cherry-stones, and pursues
them to the banks of the Rhine, in a stream of spilt
port.

Smart. Oh, damn it, he'll do.

Foote. Or what say you to your father-in-law, Sir
Timothy ? who, though as broken-winded as a Houn-
slow post-horse, is eternally chaunting Venetian bal-
lads. *Kata tore cara higlia.*

Smart. Admirable ! by Heavens !——Have you got
'em ?

Foote. No.

Smart. Then in with 'em my boy.

Foote. Not one.

Smart. Pr'ythee why not ?

Foote. Why look'e, Smart, though you are in the language of the world, my friend, yet there is one thing you, I am sure, love better than any body.

Smart. What's that?

Foote. Mischief.

Smart. No, pr'ythee——

Foote. How now am I sure that you, who so readily give up your relations, may not have some design upon me?

Smart. I don't understand you.

Foote. Why, as soon as my characters begin to circulate a little successfully, my mouth is stopped in a minute, by the clamour of your relations.——Oh, damme,—'tis a shame, it should not be,—people of distinction brought upon the stage.——And so out of compliment to your cousins, I am to be beggared for treating the public with the follies of your family, at your own request.

Smart. How can you think I would be such a dog? What the devil, then, are we to have nothing personal? Give us the actors, however.

Foote. Oh, that's stale. Besides, I think they have, of all men, the best right to complain.

Smart. How so?

Foote. Because, by rendering them ridiculous in their profession, you, at the same time, injure their pockets.——Now as to the other gentry, they have providentially something besides their understanding to rely upon; and the only injury they can receive, is,—that the whole town is then diverted with what before, was only the amusement of private parties.

Cank. Give us then a national portrait : a Scotch-man or an Irishman.

Foote. If you mean merely the dialect of the two countries, I cann't think it either a subject of satire or humour; it is an accidental unhappiness, for which a man is no more accountable, than the colour of his hair. Now affectation I take to be the true comic ob-ject. If, indeed, a North Briton, struck with a scheme of reformation, should advance from the banks of the Tweed, to teach the English the true pronuncia-tion of their own language, he would, I think, merit your laughter : nor would a Dublin mechanic, who, from heading the Liberty-boys, in a skirmish on Or-mond Quay, should think he had a right to prescribe military laws to the first commander in Europe, be a less ridiculous object.

Smart. Are there such ?

Foote. If you mean that the blunders of a few pea-sants, or the partial principles of a single scoundrel, are to stand as characteristical marks of a whole country; your pride may produce a laugh, but, be-lieve me, it is at the expence of your understanding.

Cank. Heyday, what a system is here! Laws for laughing !——And pray, sage sir, instruct us when we may laugh with propriety ?

Foote. At an old beau, a superannuated beauty, a military coward, a stuttering orator, or a gouty dancer. In short, whoever affects to be what he is not, or strives to be what he cannot, is an object worthy the poet's pen, and your mirth.

Smart. Psha, I don't know what you mean by your is nots, and cannots—damned abstruse jargon.—Ha, Canker!

Cank. Well, but if you will not give us persons, let us have things. Treat us with a modern amour, and a state intrigue, or a————

Foote. And so amuse the public ear at the expence of private peace. You must excuse me.

Cank. And with these principles, you expect to thrive on this spot?

Smart. No, no, it won't do. I tell thee the plain roast and boiled of the Theatres will never do at this table. We must have high seasoned *ragoûts*, and rich sauces.

Foote. Why, perhaps, by way of dessert, I may produce something that may hit your palate.

Smart. Your bill of fare?

Foote. What think you of one of those itinerant field Orators, who, though at declared enmity with common sense, have the address to poison the principles, and at the same time pick the pockets of half our industrious fellow subjects?

Cank. Have a care. Dangerous ground. *Ludere cum sacris,* you know.

Foote. Now I look upon it in a different manner. I consider these gentlemen in the light of public performers, like myself; and whether we exhibit at Tottenham-Court, or the Hay-Market, our purpose is the same, and the place is immaterial.

Cank. Why, indeed, if it be considered——

Foote. Nay, more, I must beg leave to assert, that ridicule is the only antidote against this pernicious poison. This is a madness that argument can never cure: and should a little wholesome severity be applied, persecution would be the immediate cry: where then can we have recourse, but to the comic muse? Perhaps, the archness and severity of her smile may redress an evil, that the laws cannot reach, or reason reclaim.

Cank. Why, if it does not cure those already distempered, it may be a means to stop the infection.

Smart. But how is your scheme conducted?

Foote. Of that you may judge. We are just going upon a repetition of the piece.——I should be glad to have your opinion.

Smart. We will give it you.

Foote. One indulgence: As you are Englishmen, I think, I need not beg, that as from necessity most of my performers are new, you will allow for their inexperience, and encourage their timidity.

Smart. But reasonable.

Foote. Come, then, prompter, begin.

Pearse. Lord, sir, we are all at a stand.

Foote. What's the matter?

Pearse. Mrs. O'Schohnesy has returned the part of the bawd; she says she is a gentlewoman, and it would be a reflection on her family to do any such thing!

Foote. Indeed!

Pearse. If it had been only a whore, says she, I should not have minded it; because no lady need be ashamed of doing that.

Foote. Well, there is no help for it; but these gentlemen must not be disappointed. Well, I'll do the character myself.   [*Exeunt.*

ACT I.   SCENE I.

Enter Sir WILLIAM WEALTHY, *and Mr.* RICHARD WEALTHY.

Sir William.

COME, come, brother, I know the world. People who have their attention eternally fixed upon one object, cann't help being a little narrow in their notions.

R. Weal. A sagacious remark that, and highly probable, that we merchants, who maintain a constant correspondence with the four quarters of the world, should know less of it than your fashionable fellows, whose whole experience is bounded by Westminster-bridge.

Sir Will. Nay, brother, as a proof that I am not blind to the benefit of travelling, George, you know, has been in Germany these four years.

R. Weal. Where he is well grounded in gaming and gluttony ; France has furnished him with fawning and flattery ; Italy equipp'd him with capriols and cantatas : and thus accomplished, my young gentleman is returned with a cargo of whores, cooks, valets de chambre, and fiddlesticks, a most valuable member of the British commonwealth.

Sir Will. You dislike then my system of education ?

R. Weal. Most sincerely.

Sir Will. The whole?

R. Weal. Every particular.

Sir Will. The early part, I should imagine, might merit your approbation.

R. Weal. Least of all. What, I suppose, because he has run the gauntlet through a public school, where, at sixteen, he had practised more vices than he would otherwise have heard of at sixty.

Sir Will. Ha, ha, prejudice!

R. Weal. Then, indeed, you removed him to the University; where, lest his morals should be mended, and his understanding improved, you fairly set him free from the restraint of the one, and the drudgery of the other, by the privileged distinction of a silk gown and a velvet cap.

Sir Will. And all these evils, you think, a city education would have prevented?

R. Weal. Doubtless.—Proverbs, proverbs, brother William, convey wholesome instruction. Idleness is the root of all evil. Regular hours, constant employment, and good example, cann't fail to form the mind.

Sir Will. Why truly, brother, had you stuck to your old civic vices, hypocrisy, couzenage, and avarice, I don't know whether I might not have committed George to your care; but you cockneys now beat us suburbians at our own weapons. What, old boy, times are changed since the date of thy indentures; when the sleek, crop-eared 'prentice used to dangle after his mistress, with the great bible under his arm, to St. Bride's, on a Sunday; bring home the text, repeat the divisions of the discourse, dine at twelve, and regale upon a gaudy day with buns and beer at Islington, or Mile End.

R. Weal. Wonderfully facetious!

Sir Will. Our modern lads are of a different metal. They have their gaming clubs in the Garden, their little lodgings, the snug depositories of their rusty swords, and occasional bag-wigs; their horses for the turf; ay, and their commissions of bankruptcy too, before they are well out of their time.

R. Weal. Infamous aspersion!

Sir Will. But the last meeting at Newmarket, Lord Lofty received at the hazard-table the identical note from the individual taylor to whom he had paid it but the day before, for a new set of liveries.

R. Weal. Invention!

Sir Will. These are anecdotes you will never meet with in your weekly travels from Cateaton-street to your boarded box in Clapham, brother.

R. Weal. And yet that boarded box, as your prodigal spendthrift proceeds, will soon be the only seat of the family.

Sir Will. May be not. Who knows what a reformation our project may produce!

R. Weal. I do. None at all.

Sir Will. Why so?

R. Weal. Because your means are ill-proportioned to their end. Were he my son, I would serve him—

Sir Will. As you have done your daughter—Discard him. But consider, I have but one.

R. Weal. That would weigh nothing with me : for, was Charlotte to set up a will of her own, and reject the man of my choice, she must expect to share the fate of her sister. I consider families as a smaller kind of kingdoms, and would have disobedience in the one as severely punished as rebellion in the other. Both cut off from their respective societies.

Sir Will. Poor Lucy ! But surely you begin to relent. Mayn't I intercede ?

R. Weal. Look'e, brother, you know my mind. I will be absolute. If I meddle with the management of your son, it is at your own request ; but if directly or indirectly you interfere with my banishment of that wilful, headstrong, disobedient hussy, all ties between us are broke ; and I shall no more remember you as a brother, than I do her as a child.

Sir Will. I have done. But to return. You think there is a probability in my plan ?

R. Weal. I shall attend the issue.

Sir Will. You will lend your aid, however ?

R. Weal. We shall see how you go on.

Enter Servant.

Serv. A letter, sir.

Sir Will. Oh, from Capias, my attorney. Who brought it ?

Serv. The person is without, sir.

Sir Will. Bid him wait. [*Reads.*]   [*Exit Serv.*

' WORTHY SIR,

' The bearer is the person I promised to procure.
I thought it was proper for you to examine him in
viva voce. So if you administer a few interrogatories,
you will find, by cross-questioning him, whether he
is a competent person to prosecute the cause you wot
of. I wish you a speedy issue: and as there can be
no default in your judgment, am of opinion it should
be carried into immediate execution. I am,

     ' Worthy Sir, *&c.*

         ' TIMOTHY CAPIAS.

' P. S. The party's name is Samuel Shift. He is
an admirable mime, or mimic, and most delectable
company; as we experience every Tuesday night at
our club, the Magpye and Horse-shoe, Fetter-lane.'

Very methodical indeed, Mr. Capias!——John—

Enter Servant.

Bid the person who brought this letter walk in.
[*Exit Servant.*] Have you any curiosity, brother?

R. Weal. Not a jot. I must to the Change. In
the evening you may find me in the counting-house,
or at Jonathan's.   [*Exit* R. Wealthy.

Sir Will. You shall hear from me.

Enter SHIFT *and Servant.*

Shut the door, John, and remember, I am not at
home. [*Exit Serv.*] You came from Mr. Capias?

Shift. I did, sir.

Sir Will. Your name, I think, is Shift?

Shift. It is, sir.

Sir Will. Did Mr. Capias drop any hint of my business with you?

Shift. None. He only said, with his spectacles on his nose, and his hand upon his chin, Sir William Wealthy is a respectable personage, and my client; he wants to retain you in a certain affair, and will open the case, and give you your brief himself: if you adhere to his instructions, and carry your cause, he is generous, and will discharge your bill without taxation.

Sir Will. Ha! ha! my friend Capias to a hair! Well, sir, this is no bad specimen of your abilities. But see that the door is fast. Now, sir, you are to—

Shift. A moment's pause, if you please. You must know, Sir William, I am a prodigious admirer of forms. Now Mr. Capias tells me, that it is always the rule to administer a retaining fee before you enter upon the merits.

Sir Will. Oh, sir, I beg your pardon!

Shift. Not that I question your generosity; but forms you know——

Sir Will. No apology, I beg. But as we are to have a closer connection, it may not be amiss, by way of introduction, to understand one another a little. Pray, sir, where was you born?

Shift. At my father's.

Sir Will. Hum!——And what was he?

Shift. A gentleman.

Sir Will. What was you bred ?

Shift. A gentleman.

Sir Will. How do you live ?

Shift. Like a gentleman.

Sir Will. Could nothing induce you to unbosom yourself ?

Shift. Look'e, Sir William, there is a kind of something in your countenance, a certain openness and generosity, a *je ne sçai quoi* in your manner, that I will unlock : You shall see me all.

Sir Will. You will oblige me.

Shift. You must know then, that Fortune, which frequently delights to raise the noblest structures from the simplest foundations; who from a taylor made a pope, from a gin-shop an empress, and many a prime minister from nothing at all, has thought fit to raise me to my present height, from the humble employment of Light your Honour——A link boy.

Sir Will. A pleasant fellow.——Who were your parents ?

Shift. I was produced, sir, by a left-handed marriage, in the language of the news-papers, between an illustrious lamp-lighter and an eminent itinerant cat and dog butcher.—Cat's meat, and dog's meat. ——I dare say, you have heard my mother, sir. But as to this happy pair I owe little besides my being, I shall drop them where they dropt me—in the street.

Sir Will. Proceed.

Shift. My first knowledge of the world I owe to a

C

school, which has produced many a great man—the
avenues of the play-house. There, sir, leaning on
my extinguished link, I learned dexterity from pick-
pockets, connivance from constables, politics and
fashions from footmen, and the art of making and
breaking a promise from their masters. Here, sirrah,
light me a-cross the kennel.——I hope your honour
will remember poor Jack.——You ragged rascal, I
have no halfpence——I'll pay you the next time I see
you——But, lack-a-day, sir, that time I saw as seldom as his tradesmen.

Sir Will. Very well.

Shift. To these accomplishments from without the
theatre, I must add one that I obtained within.

Sir Will. How did you gain admittance there?

Shift My merit, sir, that, like my link, threw a
radiance round me.——A detachment from the head
quarters here took possession, in the summer, of a
country corporation, where I did the honours of the
barn, by sweeping the stage and clipping the candles.
There my skill and address was so conspicuous, that
it procured me the same office, the ensuing winter, at
Drury-Lane, where I acquired intrepidity; the crown
of all my virtues.

Sir Will. How did you obtain that?

Shift. By my post. For I think, sir, he that dares
stand the shot of the gallery in lighting, snuffing, and
sweeping, the first night of a new play, may bid de-
fiance to the pillory, with all its customary com-
pliments.

Sir Will. Some truth in that.

Shift. But an unlucky crab-apple, applied to my right eye by a patriot gingerbread-baker from the Borough, who would not suffer three dancers from Switzerland because he hated the French, forced me to a precipitate retreat.

Sir Will. Poor devil!

Shift. Broglio and Contades have done the same. But as it happened, like a tennis-ball, I rose higher than the rebound.

Sir Will. How so?

Shift. My misfortune, sir, moved the compassion of one of our performers, a whimsical man, he took me into his service. To him I owe what I believe will make me useful to you.

Sir Will. Explain.

Shift. Why, sir, my master was remarkably happy in an art, which, however disesteemed at present, is, by Tully, reckoned amongst the perfections of an orator—mimicry.

Sir Will. Why you are deeply read, Mr. Shift!

Shift. A smattering—But as I was saying, sir, nothing came amiss to my master. Bipeds, or quadrupeds; rationals, or animals; from the clamour of the bar to the cackle of the barn-door; from the soporific twang of the tabernacle of Tottenham-Court, to the melodious bray of their long-eared brethren in Bunhill-Fields; all were objects of his imitation, and my attention. In a word, sir, for two whole years, under this professor, I studied and starved, impoverished my body, and pampered my mind; till thinking myself pretty near equal to my master, I made him one of his own bows, and set up for myself.

Sir Will. You have been successful, I hope.

Shift. Pretty well, I cann't complain. My art, sir, is a *pass-par-tout.* I seldom want employment. Let's see how stand my engagements. [*Pulls out a pocketbook.*] Hum—hum, Oh! Wednesday at Mrs. Gammut's, near Hanover-square; there, there, I shall make a meal upon the Mingotti; for her ladyship is in the opera interest; but, however, I shall revenge her cause upon her rival Mattei. Sunday evening at Lady Sustinuto's concert. Thursday I dine upon the actors, with ten Templars, at the Mitre in Fleet-street. Friday I am to give the amorous parly of two intriguing cats in a gutter, with the disturbing of a hen-roost, at Mr. Deputy Sugarsops, near the Monument. So, sir, you see my hands are full. In short, Sir William, there is not a buck or a turtle devoured within the bills of mortality, but there I may, if I please, stick a napkin under my chin.

Sir Will. I'm afraid, Mr. Shift, I must break in a little upon your engagements; but you shall not be a loser by the bargain.

Shift. Command me.

Sir Will. You can be secret as well as serviceable?

Shift. Mute as a mackrel.

Sir Will. Come hither then. If you betray me to my son———

Shift. Scalp me.

Sir Will. Enough.——You must know then, the hopes of our family are, Mr. Shift, centered in one boy.

Shift. And I warrant he is a hopeful one.

Sir Will. No interruption, I beg. George has been abroad these four years, and from his late behaviour I have reason to believe, that had a certain event happened, which I am afraid he wished,——my death———

Shift. Yes; that's natural enough.

Sir Will. Nay, pray,—there would soon be an end to an ancient and honourable family.

Shift. Very melancholy indeed. But families, like besoms, will wear to the stumps, and finally fret out, as you say.

Sir Will. Pr'ythee, peace for five minutes.

Shift. I am tongue-ty'd.

Sir Will. Now I have projected a scheme to prevent this calamity.

Shift. Ay, I should be glad to hear that.

Sir Will. I am going to tell it you.

Shift. Proceed.

Sir Will. George, as I have contrived it, shall experience all the misery of real ruin, without running the least risque.

Shift. Ay, that will be a *coup de maitre.*

Sir Will. I have prevailed upon his uncle, a wealthy citizen ———

Shift. I don't like a city plot.

Sir Will. I tell thee it is my own.

Shift. I beg pardon.

Sir Will. My brother, I say, some time since wrote him a circumstantial account of my death; upon which he is returned, in full expectation of succeeding to my estate.

Shift. Immediately.

Sir Will. No; when at age. In about three months.

Shift. I understand you.

Sir Will. Now, sir, guessing into what hands my heedless boy would naturally fall, on his return, I have, in a feigned character, associated myself with a set of rascals, who will spread every bait that can flatter folly, inflame extravagance, allure inexperience, or catch credulity. And when, by their means, he thinks himself reduced to the last extremity; lost even to the most distant hope——

Shift. What then?

Sir Will. Then will I step in like his guardian-angel, and snatch him from perdition. If mortified by misery, he becomes conscious of his errors, I have saved my son; but if, on the other hand, gratitude cann't bind, nor ruin reclaim him, I will cast him out as an alien to my blood, and trust for the support of my name and family to a remoter branch.

Shift. Bravely resolved. But what part am I to sustain in this drama?

Sir Will. Why George, you are to know, is already stript of what money he could command by two sharpers: but as I never trust them out of my sight, they cann't deceive me.

Shift. Out of your sight!

Sir Will. Why, I tell thee, I am one of the knot : an adept in their science, can slip, shuffle, cog, or cut with the best of them.

Shift. How do you escape your son's notice ?

Sir Will. His firm persuasion of my death, with the extravagance of my disguise.——Why, I would engage to elude your penetration, when I am beau'd out for the baron. But of that by and by. He has recourse, after his ill success, to the cent. per cent. gentry, the usurers, for a further supply.

Shift. Natural enough.

Sir Will. Pray do you know—I forget his name— a wrinkled old fellow, in a thread-bare coat ? He sits every morning, from twelve till two, in the left cor- ner of Lloyd's Coffee-house; and every evening, from five till eight, under the clock at the Temple- Exchange.

Shift. What, little Transfer the broker!

Sir Will. The same. Do you know him ?

Shift. Know him!—Ay, rot him. It was but last Easter Tuesday, he had me turned out at a feast, in Leather-seller's Hall, for singing ' Room for Cuck- olds' like a parrot ; and vowed it meant a reflection upon the whole body corporate.

Sir Will. You have reason to remember him.

Shift. Yes, yes, I recommended a minor to him myself, for the loan only of fifty pounds ; and would

you believe it, as I hope to be saved, we dined, sup-
ped, and wetted, five and thirty guineas upon tick, in
meetings at the Cross-keys, in order to settle the
terms ; and after all, the scoundrel would not lend us
a stiver.

Sir Will. Could you personate him ?

Shift. Him! Oh, you shall see me shift into his
shamble in a minute: and, with a withered face, a bit
of a purple nose, a cautionary stammer, and a sleek
silver head, I would undertake to deceive even his
banker. But to speak the truth, I have a friend that
can do this inimitably well. Have not you something
of more consequence for me ?

Sir Will. I have.——Could not you, master Shift,
assume another shape ? You have attended auctions.

Shift. Auctions! a constant puff. Deep in the mystery ; a professed *connoisseur*, from a Niger to a Nau-
tilus, from the Apollo Belvidere to a Butterfly.

Sir Will. One of these insinuating, oily orators I will
get you to personate: for we must have the plate and
jewels in our possession, or they will soon fall into
other hands.

Shift. I will do it.

Sir Will. Within I will give you farther instructions.

Shift. I'll follow you.

Sir Will. [*Going, returns.*] You will want mate-
rials.

Shift. Oh, m dress I can be furnished with in five
minutes. [*Exit Sir* Will.]——A whimsical old blade

this. I shall laugh if this scheme miscarries. I have
a strange mind to lend it a lift—never had a greater
———Pho, a damned unnatural connection this of
mine! What have I to do with fathers and guardians !
a parcel of preaching, prudent, careful, curmudgeonly
—dead to pleasures themselves, and the blasters of it
in others.——Mere dogs in a manger——No, no, I'll
veer, tack about, open my budget to the boy, and join
in a counter-plot. But hold, hold, friend Stephen,
see first how the land lies. Who knows whether this
Germanized genius has parts to comprehend, or spirit to reward thy merit. There's danger in that, ay,
marry is there. 'Egad, before I shift the helm, I'll
first examine the coast; and then if there be but a
bold shore, and a good bottom, have a care, old
Square Toes, you will meet with your match. [*Exit.*

Enter Sir GEORGE, LOADER, *and Servant.*

Sir Geo. Let the Martin pannels for the vis-a-vis be
carried to Long-Acre, and the pye-balls sent to Hall's
to be bitted——You will give me leave to be in your
debt till the evening, Mr. Loader.——I have just
enough left to discharge the baron; and we must, you
know, be punctual with him, for the credit of the
country.

Load. Fire him, a snub-nosed son of a bitch. Levant me, but he got enough last night to purchase a
principality amongst his countrymen, the High dutch-
ians and Hussarians.

Sir Geo. You had your share, Mr. Loader.

Load. Who, I?——Lurch me at four, but I was marked to the top of your trick, by the baron, my dear. What, I am no cinque and quarter man. Come, shall we have a dip in the history of the Four Kings this morning?

Sir Geo. Rather too early. Besides, it is the rule abroad, never to engage a-fresh, till our old scores are discharged.

Load. Capot me, but those lads abroad are pretty fellows, let them say what they will. Here, sir, they will vowel you from father to son, to the twentieth generation. They would as soon, now-a-days, pay a tradesman's bill, as a play debt. All sense of honour is gone, not a stiver stirring. They could as soon raise the dead as two pounds two; nick me, but I have a great mind to tie up, and ruin the rascals——— What, has Transfer been here this morning?

Enter DICK.

Sir Geo. Any body here this morning, Dick?

Dick. No body, your honour.

Load. Repique the rascal. He promised to be here before me.

Dick. I beg your honour's pardon. Mrs. Cole from the Piazza was here, between seven and eight.

Sir Geo. An early hour for a lady of her calling.

Dick. Mercy on me! The poor gentlewoman is mortally altered since we used to lodge there, in our jaunts from Oxford; wrapt up in flannels: all over the rheumatise.

Load. Ay, ay, old Moll is at her last stake.

Dick. She bade me say, she just stopt in her way to the tabernacle; after the exhortation, she says, she'll call again.

Sir Geo. Exhortation!——Oh, I recollect. Well, whilst they only make proselytes from that profession, they are heartily welcome to them. She does not mean to make me a convert?

Dick. I believe she has some such design upon me; for she offered me a book of hymns, a shilling, and a dram, to go along with her.

Sir Geo. No bad scheme, Dick. Thou hast a fine, sober, psalm-singing countenance; and when thou hast been some time in their trammels, may'st make as able a teacher as the best of them.

Dick. Laud, sir; I want learning.

Sir Geo. Oh, the spirit, the spirit, will supply all that, Dick, never fear.

Enter Sir WILLIAM, *as a German Baron.*

My dear baron, what news from the Hay-Market? What says the Florenza? Does she yield? Shall I be happy? Say yes, and command my fortune.

Sir Will. I was never did see so fine a woman since I was leave Hamburgh; dere was all de colour, all red and white, dat was quite natural; point d'artifice. Then she was dance and sing—— I vow to Heaven, I was never see de like!

Sir Geo. But how did she receive my embassy?— What hopes?

Sir Will. Why dere was, monsieur le chevalier, when I first enter, dree or four damned queer people; ah, ah, dought I, by gad I guess your business. Dere was one fat big woman's, dat I know long time: le valet de chambre was tell me dat she came from a grand merchand; ha, ha, dought I, by your leave, stick to your shop; or, if you must have de pritty girl, dere is de play-hous, dat do very well for you; but for de opera, pardonnez, by gar dat is meat for your master.

Sir Geo. Insolent mechanic!——But she despised him?

Sir Will. Ah, may foy, he is damned rich, has beaucoup de guineas; but after de fat woman was go, I was tell the signora, madam, dere is one certain chevalier of dis country, who has travelled, see de world, bien fait, well made, beaucoup d'Esprit, a great deal of monies, who beg, by gar, to have de honour to drow himself at your feet.

Sir Geo. Well, well, baron.

Sir Will. She aska your name; as soon as I tell her, aha, by gar, dans an instant, she melt like de lomp of sugar: she run to her bureau, and, in de minute, return wid de paper.

Sir Geo. Give it me.   [*Reads.*

Les preliminaries d'une traite entre le chevalier Wealthy, and la signor Diamenti.

A bagatelle, a trifle: she shall have it.

Load. Hark'e, knight, what is all that there outlandish stuff?

Sir Geo. Read, read ! The eloquence of angels, my dear baron !

Load. Slam me, but the man's mad ! I don't understand their gibberish——What is it in English ?

Sir Geo. The preliminaries of a subsidy treaty, between Sir G. Wealthy, and Signora Florenza. That the said signora will resign the possession of her person to the said Sir George, on the payment of three hundred guineas monthly, for equipage, table, domestics, dress, dogs, and diamonds ; her debts to be duly discharged, and a note advanced of five hundred by way of entrance.

Load. Zounds, what a cormorant ! She must be devilish handsome.

Sir Geo. I am told so.

Load. Told so ! Why, did you never see her ?

Sir Geo. No ; and possibly never may, but from my box at the opera.

Load. Hey-day ! Why what the devil—

Sir Geo. Ha, ha, you stare, I don't wonder at it. This is an elegant refinement, unknown to the gross voluptuaries of this part of the world. This is, Mr. Loader, what may be called a debt to your dignity : for an opera girl is as essential a piece of equipage for a man of fashion, as his coach.

Load. The devil !

Sir Geo. 'Tis for the vulgar only to enjoy what they possess : the distinction of ranks and conditions are, to have hounds, and never hunt ; cooks, and

D

dine at taverns ; houses, you never inhabit ; mistresses, you never enjoy——

Load. And debts, you never pay. Egad, I am not surprized at it ; if this be your trade, no wonder that you want money for necessaries, when you give such a damn'd deal for nothing at all.

Enter Servant.

Serv. Mrs. Cole, to wait upon your honour.

Sir Geo. My dear baron, run, dispatch my affair, conclude my treaty, and thank her for the very reasonable conditions.

Sir Will. I sall.

Sir Geo. Mr. Loader, shall I trouble you to introduce the lady ? She is, I think, your acquaintance.

Load. Who, old Moll ? Ay, ay, she's your market-woman. I would not give six-pence for your signoras. One armful of good, wholesome British beauty, is worth a ship-load of their trapsing, tawdry trollops. But hark'e, baron, how much for the table ? Why she must have a devilish large family, or a monstrous stomach.

Sir Will. Ay, ay, dere, is her moder, la complaisante to walk in de Park, and to go to de play ; two broders, deaux valets, dree Spanish lap-dogs, and de monkey.

Load. Strip me, if I would set five shillings against the whole gang. May my partner renounce with the game in his hand, if I were you, knight, if I would not—— [*Exit* Bar.

1

Sir Geo. But the lady waits —[*Exit* Load.]—A strange fellow this! What a whimsical jargon he talks! Not an idea abstracted from play! To say truth, I am sincerely sick of my acquaintance : But, however, I have the first people in the kingdom to keep me in countenance. Death and the dice level all distinctions.

Enter Mrs. COLE, *supported by* LOADER *and* DICK.

Mrs. Cole. Gently, gently, good Mr. Loader.

Load. Come along, old Moll. Why, you jade, you look as rosy this morning ; I must have a smack at your muns. Here, taste her, she is as good as old hock to get you a stomach.

Mrs. Cole. Fye, Mr. Loader, I thought you had forgot me.

Load. I forget you! I would as soon forget what is trumps.

Mrs. Cole. Softly, softly, young man. There, there, mighty well. And how does your honour do? I han't seen your honour, I cann't tell the— Oh! mercy on me, there's a twinge——

Sir Geo. What is the matter, Mrs. Cole?

Mrs. Cole. My old disorder, the rheumatise; I han't been able to get a wink of——Oh la! what, you have been in town these two days?

Sir Geo. Since Wednesday.

Mrs. Cole. And never once called upon old Cole. No, no, I am worn out, thrown by and forgotten, like a tattered garment, as Mr. Squintum says. Oh, he

D ij

is a dear man! But for him I had been a lost sheep ;
never known the comforts of the new birth ; no.—
There's your old friend, Kitty Carrot, at home still.
What, shall we see you this evening ? I have kept
the green room for you ever since I heard you were
in town.

Load. What shall we take a snap at old Moll's.—
Hey, beldam, have you a good batch of burgundy
abroach ?

Mrs. Cole. Bright as a ruby ; and for flavour!
You know the colonel—He and Jenny Cummins
drank three flasks, hand to fist, last night.

Load. What, and bilk thee of thy share ?

Mrs. Cole. Ah, don't mention it, Mr. Loader. No,
that's all over with me. The time has been, when I
could have earned thirty shillings a day by my own
drinking, and the next morning was neither sick nor
sorry : But now, O laud, a thimbleful turns me topsy-
turvy.

Load. Poor old girl !

Mrs. Cole. Ay, I have done with these idle vanities ;
my thoughts are fixed upon a better place. What, I
suppose, Mr. Loader, you will be for your old friend
the black-ey'd girl from Rosemary-lane. Ha, ha !
Well, 'tis a merry little tit. A thousand pities she's
such a reprobate !——But she'll mend ; her time is
not come : all shall have their call, as Mr. Squintum
says, sooner or later ; regeneration is not the work of
a day. No, no, no,—Oh !

Sir Geo. Not worse, I hope.

Mrs. Cole. Rack, rack, gnaw, gnaw, never easy, a-bed or up, all's one. Pray, honest friend, have you any clary, or mint-water in the house?

Dick. A case of French drams.

Mrs. Cole. Heaven defend me! I would not touch a dram for the world.

Sir Geo. They are but cordials, Mrs. Cole. Fetch them, you blockhead.   [*Exit* Dick.

Mrs. Cole. Ay, I am a going; a wasting, and a wasting, Sir George. What will become of the house when I am gone, Heaven knows.——No.——When people are missed, then they are mourned. Sixteen years have I lived in the Garden, comfortably and creditably; and, though I say it, could have got bail any hour of the day: reputable tradesmen, Sir George, neighbours, Mr. Loader knows; no knock-me-down doings in my house. A set of regular, sedate, sober customers. No rioters. Sixteen did I say—Ay, eighteen years I have paid scot and lot in the parish of St. Paul's, and during the whole time nobody have said, Mrs. Cole, why do you so? Unless twice that I was before Sir Thomas De Val, and three times in the round-house.

Sir Geo. Nay, don't weep, Mrs. Cole.

Load. May I lose deal, with an honour at bottom, if old Moll does not bring tears into my eyes.

Mrs. Cole. However, it is a comfort after all, to think one has pass'd through the world with credit and character. Ay, a good name, as Mr. Squintum says, is better than a gallipot of ointment.

Enter DICK, *with a Dram.*

Load. Come, haste, Dick, haste; sorrow is dry. Here, Moll, shall I fill thee a bumper?

Mrs. Cole. Hold, hold, Mr. Loader! Heaven help you, I could as soon swallow the Thames. Only a sip, to keep the gout out of my stomach.

Load. Why then, here's to thee.—Levant me, but it is supernaculum.—Speak when you have enough.

Mrs. Cole. I won't trouble you for the glass; my hands do so tremble and shake, I shall but spill the good creature.

Load. Well pulled. But now to business. Pr'ythee, Moll, did not I see a tight young wench in a linen gown knock at your door this morning?

Mrs. Cole. Ay; a young thing from the country.

Load. Could we not get a peep at her this evening?

Mrs. Cole. Impossible! She is engaged to Sir Timothy Totter. I have taken earnest for her these three months.

Load. Pho, what signifies such a fellow as that! Tip him an old trader, and give her to the knight.

Mrs. Cole. Tip him an old trader!—Mercy on us, where do you expect to go when you die, Mr. Loader?

Load. Crop me, but this Squintum has turned her brains.

Sir Geo. Nay, Mr. Loader, I think the gentleman has wrought a most happy reformation.

Mrs. Cole. Oh, it was a wonderful work. There

had I been tossing in a sea of sin, without rudder or compass. And had not the good gentleman piloted me into the harbour of grace, I must have struck against the rocks of reprobation, and have been quite swallowed up in the whirlpool of despair. He was the precious instrument of my spiritual sprinkling.— But however, Sir George, if your mind be set upon a young country thing, to-morrow night I believe I can furnish you.

Load. As how?

Mrs. Cole. I have advertised this morning in the register-office for servants under seventeen; and ten to one but I light on something that will do.

Load. Pillory me, but it has a face.

Mrs. Cole. Truly, consistently with my conscience, I would do any thing for your honour.

Sir Geo. Right, Mrs. Cole, never lose sight of that monitor. But pray how long has this heavenly change been wrought in you?

Mrs. Cole. Ever since my last visitation of the gout. Upon my first fit, seven years ago, I began to have my doubts and my waverings; but I was lost in a labyrinth, and nobody to shew me the road. One time I thought of dying a Roman, which is truly a comfortable communion enough for one of us: but it would not do.

Sir Geo. Why not?

Mrs. Cole. I went one summer over to Boulogne to repent; and, would you believe it, the bare-footed, bald-pate beggars would not give me absolution without I quitted my business——Did you ever hear of such a set of scabby——Besides, I could not bear their barbarity. Would you believe it, Mr. Loader, they lock up for their lives, in a nunnery, the prettiest, sweetest, tender, young things!——Oh, six of them, for a season, would finish my business here, and then I should have nothing to do but to think of hereafter.

Load. Brand me, what a country!

Sir Geo. Oh, scandalous!

Mrs. Cole. O no, it would not do. So, in my last illness, I was wished to Mr. Squintum, who stept in with his saving grace, got me with the new birth, and I became as you see, regenerate, and another creature.

Enter DICK.

Dick. Mr. Transfer, sir, has sent to know if your honour be at home.

Sir Geo. Mrs. Cole, I am mortified to part with you. But business, you know——

Mrs. Cole. True, Sir George, Mr. Loader, your arm——Gently, oh, oh!

Sir Geo. Would you take another thimbleful, Mrs. Cole?

Mrs. Cole. Not a drop——I shall see you this evening?

Sir Geo. Depend upon me.

Mrs. Cole. To-morrow I hope to suit you——We are to have at the tabernacle an occasional hymn, with a thanksgiving sermon for my recovery. After which, I shall call at the register-office, and see what goods my advertisement has brought in.

Sir Geo. Extremely obliged to you, Mrs. Cole.

Mrs. Cole. Or if that should not do, I have a tid bit at home will suit your stomach. Never brushed by a beard. Well, Heaven bless you—Softly, have a care, Mr. Loader——Richard, you may as well give me the bottle into the chair, for 'fear I should be taken ill on the road. Gently——so, so!

[*Exit Mrs.* Cole *and* Loader.

Sir Geo. Dick, shew Mr. Transfer in. [*Exit* Dick.] ——Ha, ha, what a hodge podge! How the jade has jumbled together the carnal and the spiritual; with what ease she reconciles her new birth to her old calling!——No wonder these preachers have plenty of proselytes, whilst they have the address so comfortably to blend the hitherto jarring interests of the two worlds.

Enter LOADER.

Load. Well, knight, I have housed her; but they want you within, sir.

Sir Geo. I'll go to them immediately.

[*Exeunt severally.*

ACT II.   SCENE I.

Enter DICK, *introducing* TRANSFER.

Dick.

MY master will come to you presently.

Enter Sir GEORGE.

Sir Geo. Mr. Transfer, your servant.

Trans. Your honour's very humble. I thought to have found Mr. Loader here.

Sir Geo. He will return immediately. Well, Mr. Transfer——but take a chair—you have had a long walk. Mr. Loader, I presume, opened to you the urgency of my business.

Trans. Ay, ay, the general cry, money, money! I don't know, for my part, where all the money is flown to. Formerly a note, with a tolerable endorsement, was as current as cash. If your uncle Richard now would join in this security——

Sir Geo. Impossible.

Trans. Ay, like enough. I wish you were of age.

Sir Geo. So do I. But as that will be considered in the premium.——

Trans. True, true,——I see you understand business——And what sum does your honour lack at present?

Sir Geo. Lack!——How much have you brought?

Trans. Who, I? Dear me! none.

Sir Geo. Zounds, none !

Trans. Lack-a-day, none to be had, I think. All the morning have I been upon the hunt. There, Ephraim Barebones, the tallow-chandler, in Thames-street, used to be a never-failing chap; not a guinea to be got there. Then I tottered away to Nebuchadnezzar Zebulon in the Old Jewry, but it happened to be Saturday; and they never touch on the sabbath, you know.

Sir Geo. Why what the devil can I do ?

Trans. Good me, I did not know your honour had been so pressed.

Sir Geo. My honour pressed! Yes, my honour is not only pressed, but ruined, unless I can raise money to redeem it. That blockhead Loader, to depend upon this old doating———

Trans. Well, well, now I declare I am quite sorry to see your honour in such a taking.

Sir Geo. Damn your sorrow.

Trans. But come, don't be cast down : though money is not to be had, money's worth may, and that's the same thing.

Sir Geo. How, dear Transfer ?

Trans Why I have at my warehouse in the city, ten casks of whale-blubber, a large cargo of Dantzic dowlas, with a curious sortment of Birmingham hafts, and Witney blankets for exportation.

Sir Geo. Hey !

Trans. And stay, stay, then, again, at my country-house, the bottom of Gray's-inn-lane, there's a hundred ton of fine old hay, only damaged a little last winter for want of thatching; with forty load of flint stones.

Sir Geo. Well.

Trans. Your honour may have all these for a rea-sonable profit, and convert them into cash.

Sir Geo. Blubber and blankets! Why, you old rascal, do you banter me?

Trans. Who I? O law, marry, Heaven forbid.

Sir Geo. Get out of my—you stuttering scoundrel.

Trans. If your honour would but hear me——

Sir Geo. Troop, I say, unless you have a mind to go a shorter way than you came. [*Exit* Trans.] And yet there is something so uncommonly ridiculous in his proposal, that were my mind more at ease——

Enter LOADER.

So, sir, you have recommended me to a fine fellow.

Load. What's the matter?

Sir Geo. He cannot supply me with a shilling! and wants, besides, to make me a dealer in dowlas.

Load. Ay, and a very good commodity too. Peo-ple that are upon ways and means, must not be nice, knight.——A pretty piece of work you have made here!——Thrown up the cards, with the game in your hands.

Sir Geo. Why, pr'ythee, of what use would his——

Load. Use! of every use. Procure you the spank-ers, my boy. I have a broker, that, in a twinkling, shall take off your bargain.

Sir Geo. Indeed!

Load. Indeed!——Ay, indeed.——You sit down to hazard and not know the chances! I'll call him back. ——Halloo, Transfer.——A pretty little, busy, bustling——You may travel miles, before you will meet with his match. If there is one pound in the city, he will get it. He creeps like a ferret into their bags, and makes the yellow boys bolt again.

Enter TRANSFER.

Come hither, little Tranfer; what, man, our Minor was a little too hasty; he did not understand trap: knows nothing of the game, my dear.

Trans. What I said was to serve Sir George; as he seemed——

Load. I told him so; well, well, we will take thy commodities, were they as many more. But try, pr'ythee, if thou couldst not procure us some of the ready for present spending.

Trans. Let me consider.

Load. Ay, do, come: shuffle thy brains; never fear the baronet. To let a lord of lands want shiners; 'tis a shame.

Trans. I do recollect, in this quarter of the town, an old friend, that used to do things in this way.

Load. Who?

Trans. Statute, the scrivener.

Load. Slam me, but he has nicked the chance.

Trans. A hard man, master Loader!

Sir Geo. No matter.

E

Trans. His demands are exorbitant.

Sir Geo. That is no fault of ours.

Load. Well said, knight!

Trans. But to save time, I had better mention his terms.

Load. Unnecessary.

Trans. Five per cent. legal interest.

Sir Geo. He shall have it.

Trans. Ten, the premium.

Sir Geo. No more words.

Trans. Then, as you are not of age, five more for insuring your life.

Load. We will give it.

Trans. As for what he will demand for the risque—

Sir Geo. He shall be satisfied.

Trans. You pay the attorney.

Sir Geo. Amply, amply; Loader, dispatch him.

Load. There, there, little Transfer; now every thing is settled. All things shall be complied with, reasonable or unreasonable. What, our principal is a man of honour. [*Exit* Trans.] Hey, my knight, this is doing business. This pinch is a sure card.

Re-enter TRANSFER.

Trans. I had forgot one thing. I am not the principal; you pay the brokerage.

Load. Ay, ay; and a handsome present into the bargain, never fear.

Trans. Enough, enough.

Load. Hark'e, Transfer, we'll take the Birmingham hafts and Witney wares.

Trans. They shall be forthcoming.——You would not have the hay with the flints?

Load. Every pebble of 'em. The magistrates of the baronet's borough are infirm and gouty. He shall deal them as new pavement. [*Exit* Trans.] So, that's settled. I believe, knight, I can lend you a helping hand as to the last article. I know some traders that will truck : fellows with finery, not commodities of such clumsy conveyance as old Transfer's.

Sir Geo. You are obliging.

Load. I'll do it, boy; and get you into the bargain, a bonny auctioneer, that shall dispose of them all in a crack. [*Exit.*

Enter DICK.

Dick. Your uncle, sir, has been waiting some time.

Sir Geo. He comes in a lucky hour. Shew him in. [*Exit* Dick.] Now for a lecture. My situation sha'n't sink my spirits, however.——Here comes the musty trader, running over with remonstrances. I must banter the cit.

Enter RICHARD WEALTHY.

R. Weal. So, sir, what, I suppose, this is a spice of your foreign breeding, to let your uncle kick his heels in your hall, whilst your presence chamber is crowded with pimps, bawds, and gamesters.

E ij

Sir Geo. Oh, a proof of my respect, dear nuncle.—
Would it have been decent now, nuncle, to have in-
troduced you into such company?

R. Weal. Wonderfully considerate!—Well, young
man, and what do you think will be the end of all
this? Here I have received by the last mail, a quire
of your draughts from abroad. I see you are deter-
mined our neighbours should taste of your magni-
ficence.

Sir Geo. Yes, I think I did some credit to my
country.

R. Weal. And how are these to be paid?

Sir Geo. That I submit to you, dear nuncle.

R. Weal. From me!——Not a souse to keep you
from the counter.

Sir Geo. Why then let the scoundrels stay. It is
their duty. I have other demands, debts of honour,
which must be discharged.

R. Weal. Here's a diabolical distinction! Here's a
prostitution of words!——Honour!——'Sdeath, that
a rascal, who has picked your pocket, shall have his
crime gilded with the most sacred distinction, and
his plunder punctually paid, whilst the industrious
mechanic, who ministers to your very wants, shall
have his debt delayed, and his demand treated as insolent.

Sir Geo. Oh! a truce to this thread-bare trumpery,
dear nuncle.

R. Weal. I confess my folly; but make yourself
easy; you won't be troubled with many more of my

visits. I own I was weak enough to design a short expostulation with you; but as we in the city know the true value of time, I shall take care not to squander away any more of it upon you.

Sir Geo. A prudent resolution.

R. Weal. One commission, however, I cannot dispense with myself from executing.——It was agreed between your father and me, that as he had but one son, and I one daughter——

Sir Geo. Your gettings should be added to his estate, and my cousin Margery and I squat down together in the comfortable state of matrimony.

R. Weal. Puppy! Such was our intention. Now his last will claims this contract.

Sir Geo. Dispatch, dear nuncle.

R. Weal. Why then, in a word, see me here demand the execution.

Sir Geo. What d'ye mean?——For me to marry Margery?

R. Weal. I do.

Sir Geo. What, moi-me?

R. Weal. You, you——Your answer, ay or no?

Sir Geo. Why then, concisely and briefly, without evasion, equivocation, or further circumlocution, ——No.

R. Weal. I am glad of it.

Sir Geo. So am I.

R. Weal. But pray, if it would not be too great a favour, what objections can you have to my daughter?

Not that I want to remove 'em, but merely out of curiosity——What objections ?

Sir Geo. None. I neither know her, have seen her,
enquired after her, or ever intend it.

R. Weal. What, perhaps, I am the stumbling
block ?

Sir Geo. You have hit it.

R. Weal. Ay, now we come to the point. Well, and
pray———

Sir Geo. Why, it is not so much a dislike to your
person, though that is exceptionable enough, but
your profession, dear nuncle, is an insuperable ob-
stacle.

R. Weal. Good lack!—And what harm has that
done, pray?

Sir Geo. Done!——So stained, polluted, and tainted
the whole mass of your blood, thrown such a blot on
your 'scutcheon, as ten regular successions can hardly
efface.

R. Weal. ·The deuce !

Sir Geo. And could you now, consistently with your
duty as a faithful guardian, recommend my union
with the daughter of a trader ?

R. Weal. Why, indeed, I ask pardon ; I am afraid
I did not weigh the matter as maturely as I ought.

Sir Geo. Oh, a horrid, barbarous scheme !

R. Weal. But then I thought her having the honour
to partake of the same flesh and blood with yourself,
might prove in some measure, a kind of fullers-

earth, to scour out the dirty spots contracted by commerce.

Sir Geo. Impossible!

R. Weal. Besides, here it has been the practice even of peers.

Sir Geo. Don't mention the unnatural intercourse! Thank Heaven, Mr. Richard Wealthy, my education has been in another country, where I have been too well instructed in the value of nobility, to think of intermixing it with the offspring of a Bourgois. Why, what apology could I make to my children, for giving them such a mother?

R. Weal. I did not think of that. Then I must despair, I am afraid.

Sir Geo. I can afford but little hopes.——Though, upon recollection——Is the Grisette pretty!

R. Weal. A parent may be partial. She is thought so.

Sir Geo. Ah la jolie petite Bourgoise!——Poor girl, I sincerely pity her. And I suppose, to procure her emersion from the mercantile mud, no consideration would be spared.

R. Weal. Why, to be sure, for such an honour, one would strain a point.

Sir Geo. Why then, not totally to destroy your hopes, I do recollect an edict in favour of Britanny; that when a man of distinction engages in commerce his nobility is suffered to sleep.

R. Weal. Indeed!

Sir Geo. And upon his quitting the contagious con-
nexion, he is permitted to resume his rank.

R. Weal. That's fortunate.

Sir Geo. So, nuncle Richard, if you will sell out of
the stocks, shut up your counting house, and quit St.
Mary Ax for Grosvenor-Square——

R. Weal. What then?

Sir Geo. Why, when your rank has had time to
rouse itself, for I think your nobility, nuncle, has had
a pretty long nap, if the girl's person is pleasing, and
the purchase-money is adequate to the honour, I may
in time be prevailed upon to restore her to the right
of her family.

R. Weal. Amazing condescension!

Sir Geo. Good-nature is my foible. But, upon my
soul, I would not have gone so far for any body else.

R. Weal. I can contain no longer. Hear me, spendthrift, prodigal, do you know, that in ten days your
whole revenue won't purchase you a feather to adorn
your empty head?——

Sir Geo. Heyday, what's the matter now?

R. Weal. And that you derive every acre of your
boasted patrimony from your great uncle, a soap-
boiler!

Sir Geo. Infamous aspersion!

R. Weal. It was his bags, the fruits of his honest
industry, that preserved your lazy, beggarly nobility.
His wealth repaired your tottering hall, from the ruins
of which, even the rats had run.

Sir Geo. Better our name had perished! Insupportable! soap-boiling, uncle!

R. Weal. Traduce a trader in a country of commerce! It is treason against the community; and, for your punishment, I would have you restored to the sordid condition from whence we drew you, and like your predecessors, the Picts, stript, painted, and fed upon hips, haws, and blackberries.

Sir Geo. A truce, dear haberdasher.

R. Weal. One pleasure I have, that to this gaol you are upon the gallop; but have a care, the sword hangs but by a thread. When next we meet, know me for the master of your fate.   [*Exit.*

Sir Geo. Insolent mechanic! But that his Bourgois blood would have soil'd my sword———

Enter Sir WILLIAM, *and* LOADER.

Sir Will. What is de matter?

Sir Geo. A fellow, here, upon the credit of a little affinity, has dared to upbraid me with being sprung from a soap-boiler.

Sir Will. Vat, you from the boiler of soap!

Sir Geo. Me.

Sir Will. Aha, begar, dat is anoder ting.——And harka you, mister monsieur, ha——how dare a you have d'affrontary———

Sir Geo. How!

Sir Will. De impertinence to sit down, play wid me?

Sir Geo. What is this?

Sir Will. A beggarly Bourgois vis-a-vis, a baron of twenty descents.

Load. But baron————

Sir Will. Bygar, I am almost ashamed to win of such a low, dirty——Give me my monies, and let me never see your face.

Load. Why, but baron, you mistake this thing, I know the old buck this fellow prates about.

Sir Will. May be.

Load. Pigeon me, as true a gentleman as the grand signior. He was, indeed, a good-natured, obliging, friendly fellow; and being a great judge of soap, tar, and train-oil, he used to have it home to his house, and sell it to his acquaintance for ready money, to serve them.

Sir Will. Was dat all?

Load. Upon my honour.

Sir Will. Oh, dat, dat is anoder ting. Bygar I was afraid he was negotiant.

Load. Nothing like it.

Enter DICK.

Dick. A gentleman to enquire for Mr. Loader.

Load. I come—A pretty son of a bitch, this baron! pimps for the man, picks his pocket, and then wants to kick him out of company, because his uncle was an oilman.   [*Exit.*

Sir Will. I beg pardon, chevalier, I was mistake.

Sir Geo. Oh, don't mention it : had the slam been fact, your behaviour was natural enough.

Enter LOADER.

Load. Mr. Smirk, the auctioneer.

Sir Geo. Shew him in, by all means. [*Exit* Load.

Sir Will. You have affair.

Sir Geo. If you'll walk into the next room, they will be finished in five minutes.

Enter LOADER, *with* SHIFT *as* SMIRK.

Load. Here, master Smirk, this is the gentleman. Hark'e, knight, did I not tell you, old Moll was your mark ? Here she has brought a pretty piece of man's meat already ; as sweet as a nosegay, and as ripe as a cherry, you rogue. Dispatch him, mean time we'll manage the girl. [*Exit.*

Smirk. You are the principal.

Sir Geo. Even so. I have, Mr. Smirk, some things of a considerable value, which I want to dispose of immediately.

Smirk. You have ?

Sir Geo. Could you assist me ?

Smirk. Doubtless.

Sir Geo. But directly ?

Smirk. We have an auction at twelve. I'll add your cargo to the catalogue.

Sir Geo. Can that be done ?

Smirk. Every day's practice: it is for the credit of the sale. Last week, amongst the valuable effects of a gentleman, going abroad, I sold a choice collection of china, with a curious service of plate ; though the real party was never master of above two delft dishes, and a dozen of pewter, in all his life.

Sir Geo. Very artificial. But this must be concealed.

Smirk. Buried here. Oh, many an aigrette and solitaire have I sold, to discharge a lady's play-debt. But then we must know the parties; otherwise it might be knock'd down to the husband himself. Ha, ha——Hey ho!

Sir Geo. True. Upon my word, your profession requires parts.

Smirk. No body's more. Did you ever hear, Sir George, what first brought me into the business?

Sir Geo. Never.

Smirk. Quite an accident, as I may say. You must have known my predecessor, Mr. Prig, the greatest man in the world, in his way, ay, or that ever was, or ever will be; quite a jewel of a man; he would touch you up a lot; there was no resisting him. He would force you to bid, whether you would or no. I shall never see his equal.

Sir Geo. You are modest, Mr. Smirk.

Smirk. No, no, but his shadow. Far be it from me, to vie with great men. But as I was saying, my predecessor, Mr. Prig, was to have a sale as it might be on a Saturday. On Friday at noon, I shall never forget the day, he was suddenly seized with a violent cholic. He sent for me to his bed-side, squeezed me by the hand; Dear Smirk, said he, what an accident! You know what is to-morrow; the

greatest shew this season ; prints, pictures, bronzes,
butterflies, medals, and minionettes; all the world will
be there; Lady Dy Joss, Mrs. Nankyn, the Dutchess of
Dupe, and every body at all: You see my state, it
will be impossible for me to mount. What can I do ?
—It was not for me, you know, to advise that great
man.

Sir Geo. No, no.

Smirk. At last looking wishfully at me, Smirk, says
he, d'you love me ?—Mr. Prig, can you doubt it ?—
I'll put it to the test, says he ; supply my place, to-
morrow.—I, eager to shew my love, rashly and
rapidly replied, 1 will.

Sir Geo. That was bold.

Smirk. Absolute madness. But I had gone too far
to recede. Then the point was, to prepare for the
awful occasion. The first want that occurred to me,
was a wig ; but this was too material an article to depend on my own judgment. I resolved to consult
my friends. I told them the affair————You hear,
gentlemen, what has happened ; Mr. Prig, one of the
greatest men in his way, the world ever saw, or ever
will, quite a jewel of a man, taken with a violent fit
of the cholic; to-morrow, the greatest shew this season;
prints, pictures, bronzes. butterflies, medals, and minionettes ; every body in the world to be there ; Lady Dy
Joss, Mrs. Nankyn, Dutchess of Dupe, and all mankind ; it being impossible he should mount, I have
consented to sell————They stared—it is true, gentlemen. Now I should be glad to have your opinions

F

as to a wig. They were divided : some recommended
a tye, others a bag : one mentioned a bob, but was
soon over-ruled. Now, for my part, I own, I rather
inclined to the bag; but to avoid the imputation of
rashness, I resolved to take Mrs. Smirk's judgment,
my wife, a dear good woman, fine in figure, high in
taste, a superior genius, and knows old china like a
Nabob.

Sir Geo. What was her decision ?

Smirk. I told her the case—My dear, you know
what has happened. My good friend, Mr. Prig, the
greatest man in the world, in his way, that ever was,
or ever will be, quite a jewel of a man, a violent fit of
the cholic———the greatest shew this season, to-
morrow, pictures, and every thing in the world ; all
the world will be there: now, as it is impossible he
should, I mount in his stead. You know the import-
ance of a wig : I have asked my friends—some recommended a tye, others a bag—what is your opinion ?
Why, to deal freely, Mr. Smirk, says she, a tye for
your round, regular, smiling face would be rather too
formal, and a bag too boyish, deficient in dignity for
the solemn occasion; were I worthy to advise, you
should wear a something between both. I'll be hanged,
if you don't mean a major. I jumped at the hint, and
a major it was.

Sir Geo. So, that was fixt.

Smirk. Finally. But next day, when I came to mount
the rostrum, then was the trial. My limbs shook, and
my tongue trembled. The first lot was a chamber-

utensil, in Chelsea china, of the pea-green pattern.
It occasioned a great laugh; but I got through it. Her
grace, indeed, gave me great encouragement. I overheard her whisper to Lady Dy, Upon my word, Mr.
Smirk does it very well. Very well, indeed, Mr. Smirk,
addressing herself to me. I made an acknowledging
bow to her grace, as in duty bound. But one flower
flounced involuntarily from me that day, as I may say.
I remember, Dr. Trifle called it enthusiastic, and
pronounced it a presage of my future greatness.

Sir Geo. What was that?

Smirk. Why, sir, the lot was a Guido; a single
figure, a marvellous fine performance; well preserved,
and highly finished. It stuck at five and forty: I,
charmed with the picture, and piqued at the people,
A going for five and forty, no body more than five
and forty?——Pray, ladies and gentlemen, look at
this piece, quite flesh and blood, and only wants a
touch from the torch of Prometheus, to start from
the canvass and fall a bidding. A general plaudit
ensued, I bowed, and in three minutes knocked it
down at sixty-three, ten.

Sir Geo. That was a stroke at least equal to your
master.

Smirk. O dear me! You did not know the great
man, alike in every thing. He had as much to say
upon a ribbon as a Raphael. His manner was inimitably fine. I remember they took him off at the play-
house, some time ago; pleasant, but wrong. Public

characters should not be sported with—They are sacred.——But we lose time.

Sir Geo. Oh, in the lobby on the table, you will
find the particulars.

Smirk. We shall see you, there will be a world of
company. I shall please you. But the great nicety
of our art is, the eye. Mark how mine skims round
the room. Some bidders are shy, and only advance
with a nod ; but I nail them. One, two, three, four,
five. You will be surprised—Ha, ha, ha !—Heigh
ho !   [*Exit.*

ACT III. SCENE I.

Enter Sir GEORGE, *and* LOADER.

Sir George.

A MOST infernal run. Let's see, [*Pulls out a card.*]
Loader a thousand, the baron two, Tally——Enough
to beggar a banker. Every shilling of Transfer's
supply exhausted ! nor will even the sale of my move-
ables prove sufficient to discharge my debts. Death
and the devil ! In what a complication of calamities
has a few days plunged me ! And no resource !

Load. Knight, here's old Moll come to wait on you ;
she has brought the tid-bit I spoke of. Shall I bid
her send her in ?

Sir Geo. Pray do,   [*Exit* Loader.

Enter Mrs. COLE, *and* LUCY.

Mrs. Cole. Come along, Lucy. You bashful bag-
gage, I thought I had silenced your scruples. Don't
you remember what Mr. Squintum said ? A woman's
not worth saving, that won't be guilty of a swinging
sin ; for then they have matter to repent upon. Here,
your honour, I leave her to your management. She
is young, tender, and timid ; does not know what is
for her own good : but your honour will soon teach
her. I would willingly stay, but I must not lose the
lecture.   [*Exit.*

Sir Geo. Upon my credit, a fine figure ! Awkward
——Cann't produce her publicly as mine ; but she
will do for private amusement—Will you be seated,
miss ?——Dumb! quite a picture ! she too wants a
touch of the Promethean torch—Will you be so kind,
ma'am, to walk from your frame and take a chair ?
——Come, pr'ythee, why so coy ? Nay, I am not
very adroit in the custom of this country. I suppose
I must conduct you——Come, miss.

Lucy. O, sir.

Sir Geo. Child !

Lucy. If you have any humanity, spare me.

Sir Geo. In tears ! what can this mean ? Artifice.
A project to raise the price, I suppose Look'e, my
dear, you may save this piece of pathetic for another
occasion. It won't do with me ; I am no novice——
So, child, a truce to your tragedy, I beg.

Lucy. Indeed you wrong me, sir ; indeed you do.

Sir Geo. Wrong you! how came you here, and for what purpose?

Lucy. A shameful one. I know it all, and yet believe me, sir, I am innocent.

Sir Geo. Oh, I don't question that. Your pious patroness is a proof of your innocence.

Lucy What can I say to gain your credit? And yet, sir, strong as appearances are against me, by all that's holy, you see me here, a poor distrest involuntary victim.

Sir Geo. Her stile's above the common class; her tears are real.—Rise, child.—How the poor creature trembles!

Lucy. Say then I am safe.

Sir Geo. Fear nothing.

Lucy. May heaven reward you. I cannot.

Sir Geo. Pr'ythee, child, collect yourself, and help me to unravel this mystery. You came hither willingly? There was no force?

Lucy. None.

Sir Geo. You know Mrs. Cole.

Lucy. Too well.

Sir Geo. How came you then to trust her?

Lucy. Mine, sir is a tedious, melancholy tale.

Sir Geo. And artless too?

Lucy. As innocence.

Sir Geo. Give it me.

Lucy. It will tire you.

Sir Geo. Not if it be true. Be just, and you will find me generous.

Lucy. On that, sir, I relied in venturing hither.

Sir Geo. You did me justice. Trust me with all your story. If you deserve, depend upon my protection.

Lucy. Some months ago, sir, I was considered as the joint heiress of a respectable wealthy merchant; dear to my friends, happy in my prospects, and my father's favourite.

Sir Geo. His name.

Lucy. There you must pardon me. Unkind and cruel though he has been to me, let me discharge the duty of a daughter, suffer in silence, nor bring reproach on him who gave me being.

Sir Geo. I applaud your piety.

Lucy. At this happy period, my father, judging an addition of wealth must bring an increase of happiness, resolved to unite me with a man sordid in his mind, brutal in his manners, and riches his only recommendation. My refusal of this ill-suited match, though mildly given, enflamed my father's temper, naturally choleric, alienated his affections, and banished me his house, distrest and destitute.

Sir Geo. Would no friend receive you?

Lucy. Alas, how few are friends to the unfortunate! Besides, I knew, sir, such a step would be considered by my father as an appeal from his justice. I therefore retired to a remote corner of the town, trusting, as my only advocate, to the tender calls of nature in his cool reflecting hours.

Sir Geo. How came you to know this woman?

Lucy. Accident placed me in a house, the mistress of which professed the same principles with my infamous conductress. There, as enthusiasm is the child of melancholy, I caught the infection. A constant attendance on their assemblies procured me the acquaintance of this woman, whose extraordinary zeal and devotion first drew my attention and confidence. I trusted her with my story, and in return, received the warmest invitation to take the protection of her house. This I unfortunately accepted.

Sir Geo. Unfortunately indeed!

Lucy. By the decency of appearances, I was some time imposed upon. But an accident, which you will excuse my repeating, revealed all the horror of my situation. I will not trouble you with a recital of all the arts used to seduce me: happily they hitherto have failed. But this morning I was acquainted with my destiny; and no other election left me, but immediate compliance or a jail. In this desperate condition, you cannot wonder, sir, at my choosing rather to rely on the generosity of a gentleman, than the humanity of a creature insensible to pity, and void of every virtue.

Sir Geo. The event shall justify your choice. You have my faith and honour for your security. For though I cannot boast of my own goodness, yet I have an honest feeling for afflicted virtue; and, however unfashionable, a spirit that dares afford it protection. Give me your hand. As soon as I have dispatched some pressing business here, I will lodge

you in an asylum, sacred to the distresses of your
sex ; where indigent beauty is guarded from temp-
tations, and deluded innocence rescued from infamy.

[*Exeunt.*

Enter SHIFT.

Shift. Zooks, I have toiled like a horse ; quite
tired, by Jupiter. And what shall I get for my pains ?
The old fellow here talks of making me easy for
life. Easy ! And what does he mean by easy ? He'll
make me an exciseman, I suppose; and so with an
ink-horn at my button-hole, and a taper switch in
my hand, I shall run about gauging of beer-barrels.
No, that will never do. This lad here is no fool.
Foppish, indeed. He does not want parts, no, nor
principles neither. I overheard his scene with the
girl. I think I may trust him. I have a great mind
to venture it. It is a shame to have him duped by
this old don. It must not be, I'll in and unfold——
Ha !—Egad, I have a thought too, which, if my heir
apparent can execute, I shall still lie concealed, and
perhaps be rewarded on both sides.

I have it,—'tis engender'd, piping hot,
And now, Sir Knight, I'll match you with a plot.

[Exit.

Enter Sir WILLIAM, *and* RICHARD WEALTHY.

R. Weal. Well, I suppose by this time you are satisfied what a scoundrel you have brought into the
world, and are ready to finish your foolery.

Sir Will. Got to the catastrophe, good brother.

R. Weal. Let us have it over then.

Sir Will. I have already alarmed all his tradesmen. I suppose we shall soon have him here, with a legion of bailiffs and constables.——Oh, you have my will about you?

R. Weal. Yes, yes.

Sir Will. It is almost time to produce it, or read him the clause that relates to his rejecting your daughter. That will do his business. But they come. I must return to my character.

Enter SHIFT.

Shift. Sir, sir, we are all in the wrong box; our scheme is blown up; your son has detected Loader and Tally, and is playing the very devil within.

Sir Will. Oh, the bunglers!

Shift. Now for it, youngster.

Enter Sir GEORGE, *driving in* LOADER *and another.*

Sir Geo. Rascals, robbers, that, like the locust, mark the road you have taken, by the ruin and desolation you leave behind you.

Load. Sir George!

Sir Geo. And can youth, however cautious, be guarded against such deep-laid, complicated villany? Where are the rest of your diabolical crew? your auctioneer, usurer, and——O sir, are you here?—— I am glad you have not escaped us, however.

Sir Will. What de devil is de matter?

Sir Geo. Your birth, which I believe an imposition, preserves you, however, from the discipline those rogues have received. A baron, a nobleman, a sharper! O shame! It is enough to banish all confidence from the world. On whose faith can we rely, when those, whose honour is held as sacred as an oath, unmindful of their dignity, descend to rival pick-pockets in their infamous arts. What are these [*Pulls out dice.*] pretty implements? The fruits of your leisure hours! They are dexterously done. You have a fine mechanical turn.——Dick, secure the door.

Mrs. COLE, *speaking as entering.*

Mrs. Cole. Here I am, at last. Well, and how is your honour, and the little gentlewoman?——Bless me! what is the matter here?

Sir Geo. I am, madam, treating your friends with a cold collation, and you are opportunely come for your share. The little gentlewoman is safe, and in much better hands than you designed her. Abominable hypocrite! who, tottering under the load of irreverent age and infamous diseases, inflexibly proceed in the practice of every vice, impiously prostituting the most sacred institutions to the most infernal purposes.

Mrs. Cole. I hope your honour——

Sir Geo. Take her away. As you have been singular in your penitence, you ought to be distinguished in your penance; which, I promise you, shall be most publicly and plentifully bestowed.

[*Exit Mrs.* Cole.

Enter DICK.

Dick. The constables, sir.

Sir Geo. Let them come in, that I may consign these gentlemen to their care. [*To Sir* Will.] Your letters of nobility you will produce in a court of justice. Though, if I read you right, you are one of those indigent, itinerant nobles of your own creation, which our reputation for hospitality draws hither in shoals, to the shame of our understanding, the impairing of our fortunes, and, when you are trusted, the betraying of our designs. Officers, do your duty.

Sir Will. Why, don't you know me?

Sir Geo. Just as I guessed. An impostor. He has recovered the free use of his tongue already.

Sir Will. Nay, but George.

Sir Geo. Insolent familiarity! away with him.

Sir Will. Hold, hold a moment. Brother Richard, set this matter to rights.

R. Weal. Don't you know him?

Sir Geo. Know him! The very question is an affront.

R. Weal. Nay, I don't wonder at it. 'Tis your father, you fool.

Sir Geo. My father! Impossible!

Sir Will. That may be, but 'tis true.

Sir Geo. My father alive! Thus let me greet the blessing.

Sir Will. Alive! Ay, and I believe I sha'n't be in a hurry to die again.

Sir Geo. But, dear sir, the report of your death—and this disguise——to what———

Sir Will. Don't ask any questions. Your uncle will tell you all. For my part, I am sick of the scheme.

R. Weal. I told you what would come of your politics.

Sir Will. You did so. But if it had not been for those clumsy scoundrels, the plot was as good a plot ——O, George! such discoveries I have to make.— Within I'll unravel the whole.

Sir Geo. Perhaps, sir, I may match 'em.

Shift. Sir.   [*Pulls him by the sleeve.*

Sir Geo. Never fear. It is impossible, gentlemen, to determine your fate, till this matter is more fully explained; till when, keep 'em in safe custody.——Do you know them, sir?

Sir Will. Yes, but that's more than they did me. I can cancel your debts there, and, I believe, prevail on those gentlemen to refund too——But you have been a sad profligate young dog, George.

Sir Geo. I cann't boast of my goodness, sir, but I think I could produce you a proof, that I am not so totally destitute of——

Sir Will. Ay! Why then pr'ythee do.

Sir Geo. I have, sir, this day, resisted a temptation,

that greater pretenders to morality might have yielded to.——But I will trust myself no longer, and must crave your interposition and protection.

Sir Will. To what?

Sir Geo. I will attend you with the explanation in an instant.   [*Exit.*

Sir Will Pr'ythee, Shift, what does he mean?

Shift. I believe I can guess.

Sir Will. Let us have it.

Shift I suppose the affair I overheard just now, a prodigious fine elegant girl, faith, that, discarded by her family for refusing to marry her grandfather, fell into the hands of the venerable lady you saw, who being the kind caterer for your son's amusements, brought her hither for a purpose obvious enough.—— But the young gentleman, touched with her story, truth, and tears, was converted from the spoiler of her honour to the protector of her innocence.

Sir Will. Look'e there, brother, did not I tell you that George was not so bad at the bottom!

R. Weal. This does indeed atone for half the——— But they are here.

Enter Sir GEORGE *and* LUCY.

Sir Geo. Fear nothing, madam, you may safely rely on the——

Lucy. My father!

R. Weal. Lucy!

Lucy. O, sir, can you forgive your poor distrest unhappy girl? You scarce can guess how hardly I've

been used, since my banishment from your paternal
roof.   Want, pining want, anguish and shame, have
been my constant partners.

Sir Will. Brother !

Sir Geo. Sir !

Lucy. Father !

R. Weal. Rise, child, 'tis I must ask thee forgive-
ness.   Canst thou forget the woes I've made thee suffer ? Come to my arms once more, thou darling of
my age.—What mischief had my rashness nearly
compleated.   Nephew, I scarce can thank you as I
ought, but——

Sir Geo. I am richly paid, in being the happy instrument——Yet might I urge a wish——

R. Weal. Name it.

Sir Geo. That you would forgive my follies of to-
day ; and, as I have been providentially the occasional guardian of your daughter's honour, that you
would bestow on me that right for life.

R. Weal. That must depend on Lucy ; her will,
not mine, shall now direct her choice—What says
your father ?

Sir Will. Me ! Oh, I'll shew you in an instant.—
Give me your hands.   There children, now you are
joined, and the devil take him that wishes to part
you.

Sir Geo. I thank you for us both.

R. Weal. May happiness attend you.

Sir Will. Now, brother, I hope you will allow me

to be a good plotter. All this was brought to bear by my means.

Shift. With my assistance, I hope you'll own, sir.

Sir Will. That's true, honest Shift, and thou shalt be richly rewarded ; nay, George shall be your friend too. This Shift is an ingenious fellow, let me tell you, son.

Sir Geo. I am no stranger to his abilities, sir. But, if you please, we will retire. The various struggles of this fair sufferer require the soothing softness of a sister's love. And now, sir, I hope your fears for me are over ; for had I not this motive to restrain my follies, yet I now know the town too well to be ever its bubble, and will take care to preserve, at least,

Some more estate, and principles, and wit,
Than brokers, bawds, and gamesters shall think fit.

SHIFT *addressing himself to Sir* GEORGE.

And what becomes of your poor servant Shift ?
Your father talks of lending me a lift——
A great man's promise, when his turn is serv'd !
Capons on promises wou'd soon be starv'd :
No, on myself alone, I'll now rely :
'Gad I've a thriving traffic in my eye——
Near the mad mansions of Moorfields I'll bawl ;
Friends, fathers, mothers, sisters, sons, and all,
Shut up your shops, and listen to my call.
With labour, toil, all second means dispense,
And live a rent-charge upon Providence.

Prick up your ears ; a story now I'll tell,
Which once a widow, and her child befel,
I knew the mother, and her daughter well ;
Poor, it is true, they were ; but never wanted,
For whatsoe'er they ask'd, was always granted :
One fatal day, the matron's truth was try'd,
She wanted meat and drink, and fairly cry'd.
[Child.] *Mother, you cry !* [Moth.] *Oh, child, I've got*
       no bread.

[Child.] *What matters that ? Why Providence an't dead!*
With reason good, this truth the child might say,
For there came in at noon, that very day,
Bread, greens, potatoes, and a leg of mutton,
A better sure a table ne'er was put on :
Ay, that might be, ye cry, with those poor souls ;
But we ne'er had a rasher for the coals.
And d'ye deserve it ? How d'ye spend your days ?
In pastimes, prodigality, and plays !
Let's go see Foote ! ah, Foote's a precious limb !
Old-nick will soon a foot-ball make of him !
For foremost rows in side-boxes you shove,
Think you to meet with side-boxes above ?
Where gigling girls and powder'd fops may sit,
No, you will all be cramm'd into the pit,
And croud the house for Satan's benefit.
Oh, what you snivel ? well, do so no more,
Drop, to atone, your money at the door,
And, if I please——I'll give it to the poor.

                     [Exeunt omnes.

THE END.

AUTHOR/TITLE INDEX

Note to the Reader

These indexes cover the entire Bell's series. Roman numerals refer to the set in which the individual play appears, as follows: (I) Bell's British Theatre, 1776-1781; (II) Farces, 1784; (III) Selected Plays, 1791-1802 (and 1797). Arabic numerals indicate the volume number within each of the series.

AUTHOR/TITLE INDEX

TITLE/AUTHOR INDEX

TITLE/AUTHOR INDEX